PHILIP'S

STREet

Cambridge

First published 2005 by

Philip's, a division of
Octopus Publishing Group Ltd
2–4 Heron Quays
London E14 4JP

First edition 2005
First impression 2005

ISBN-10 0-540-08854-4
ISBN-13 978-0-540-08854-6
© Philip's 2005

Ordnance Survey®

This product includes mapping data licensed from Ordnance Survey®, with the permission of the Controller of Her Majesty's Stationery Office.© Crown copyright 2005. All rights reserved.
Licence number 100011710

No part of this publication may be reproduced, stored in a retrieval system or transmitted in any form or by any means, electronic, mechanical, photocopying, recording or otherwise, without the permission of the Publishers and the copyright owner.

To the best of the Publishers' knowledge, the information in this atlas was correct at the time of going to press. No responsibility can be accepted for any errors or their consequences.

The representation in this atlas of a road, track or path is no evidence of the existence of a right of way.

Ordnance Survey and the OS symbol are registered trademarks of Ordnance Survey, the national mapping agency of Great Britain

Photographic acknowledgements:
East of England Tourist Board

Printed and bound in Spain
by Cayfosa-Quebecor.

Contents

II	**Key to map symbols**
III	**Key to map pages**
IV	**Route planning**
VI	**Sights of Cambridge**
2	**Street maps** at 4½ inches to 1 mile
44	**Street maps of Cambridge city centre** at 7 inches to 1 mile
46	**Index**
55	**List of numbered locations**

Key to map symbols

Roads

(12)	**Motorway** with junction number
A42	**Primary route** – dual/single carriageway
A42	**A road** – dual/single carriageway
B1289	**B road** – dual/single carriageway
	Through-route – dual/single carriageway
	Minor road – dual/single carriageway
	Rural track, private road or narrow road in urban area
	Path, bridleway, byway open to all traffic, road used as a public path
	Road under construction
	Pedestrianised area
	Gate or obstruction to traffic restrictions may not apply at all times or to all vehicles
P P&R	**Parking, Park and Ride**

Railways

- Railway
- Miniature railway
- Metro station, private railway station

Emergency services

- Ambulance station, coastguard station
- Fire station, police station
- Hospital, Accident and Emergency entrance to hospital

General features

- **Place of worship**, Post Office
- **Information centre** (open all year)
- Bus, coach station
- **Important buildings**, schools, colleges, universities and hospitals
- Woods, built-up area
- *Tumulus* FORT **Non-Roman antiquity, Roman antiquity**

Leisure facilities

- Camping site, caravan site
- Golf course, picnic site

Boundaries

- Postcode boundaries
- County and unitary authority boundaries

Water features

- River Ouse — **Tidal water**, water name
- **Non-tidal water** – lake, river, canal or stream
- **Lock, weir**

Enlarged mapping only

- Railway or bus station building
- Place of interest
- Parkland

Scales

Blue pages: 4½ inches to 1 mile 1:14 080
0 — 220 yds — ¼ mile — 660 yds — ½ mile
0 — 125m — 250m — 375m — ½ km

Red pages: 7 inches to 1 mile 1:9051
0 — 110 yds — 220 yds — 330 yds — ¼ mile
0 — 125m — 250m — 375m — ½ km

44 — **Adjoining page indicators** The colour of the arrow and the band indicates the scale of the adjoining page (see above)

Abbreviations

Acad	Academy	Mkt	Market
Allot Gdns	Allotments	Meml	Memorial
Cemy	Cemetery	Mon	Monument
C Ctr	Civic Centre	Mus	Museum
CH	Club House	Obsy	Observatory
Coll	College	Pal	Royal Palace
Crem	Crematorium	PH	Public House
Ent	Enterprise	Recn Gd	Recreation Ground
Ex H	Exhibition Hall	Resr	Reservoir
Ind Est	Industrial Estate	Ret Pk	Retail Park
IRB Sta	Inshore Rescue Boat Station	Sch	School
		Sh Ctr	Shopping Centre
Inst	Institute	TH	Town Hall/House
Ct	Law Court	Trad Est	Trading Estate
L Ctr	Leisure Centre	Univ	University
LC	Level Crossing	Wks	Works
Liby	Library	YH	Youth Hostel

Key to map pages

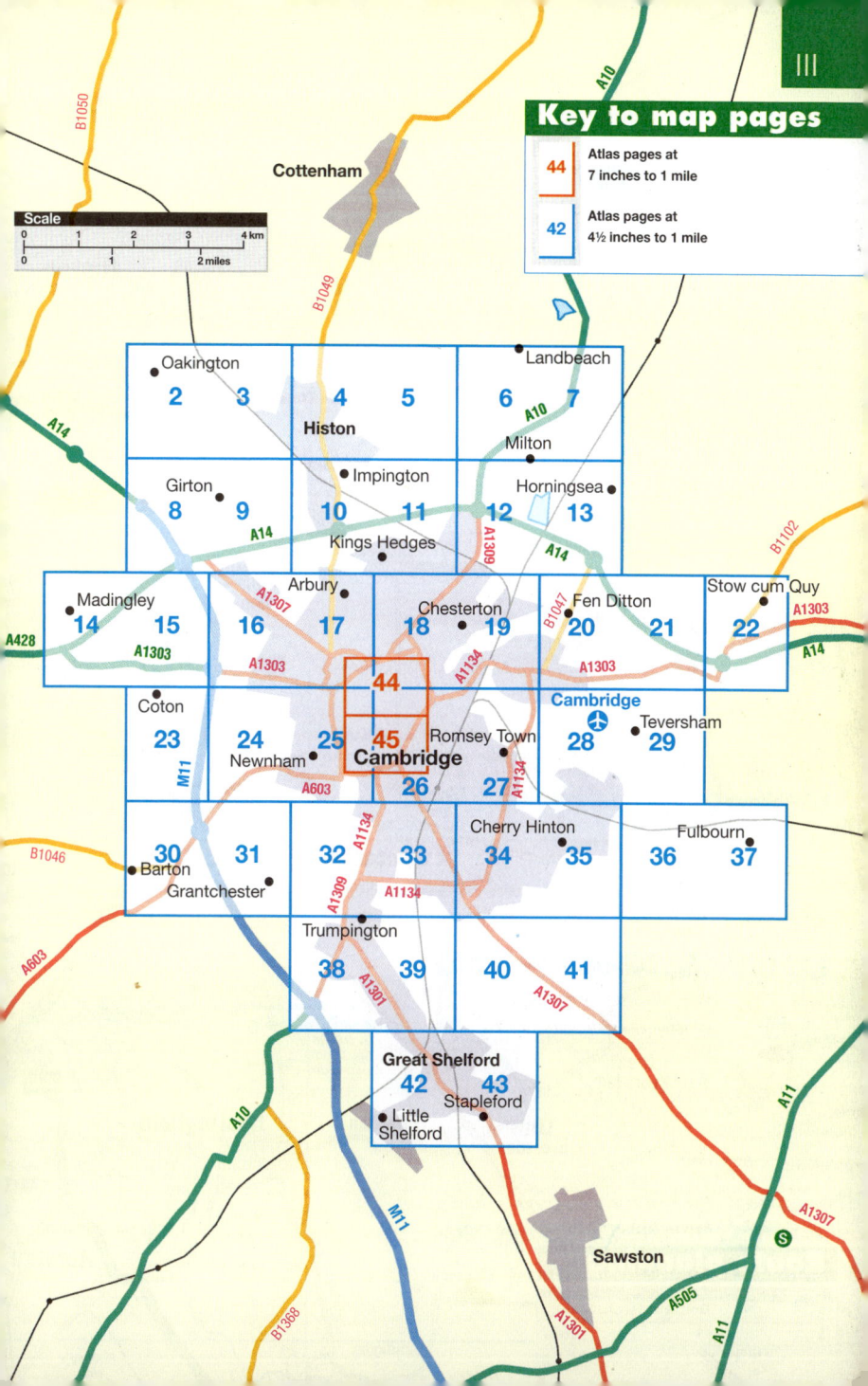

44	Atlas pages at 7 inches to 1 mile
42	Atlas pages at 4½ inches to 1 mile

Scale: 0–4 km / 0–2 miles

Cottenham

Oakington — 2, 3
Histon — 4, 5
Landbeach — 6, 7
Milton
Girton — 8, 9
Impington — 10, 11
Horningsea — 12, 13
Kings Hedges
Arbury — 16, 17
Chesterton — 18, 19
Fen Ditton — 20, 21
Stow cum Quy — 22
Madingley — 14, 15
Coton — 23
Newnham — 24, 25
Cambridge — 44, 45, 26
Romsey Town
Cambridge (airport) — 28
Teversham — 29
Barton — 30
Grantchester — 31
32, 33
Cherry Hinton — 34, 35
Fulbourn — 36, 37
Trumpington — 38, 39
40, 41
Great Shelford — 42
Little Shelford
Stapleford — 43
Sawston

Route planning

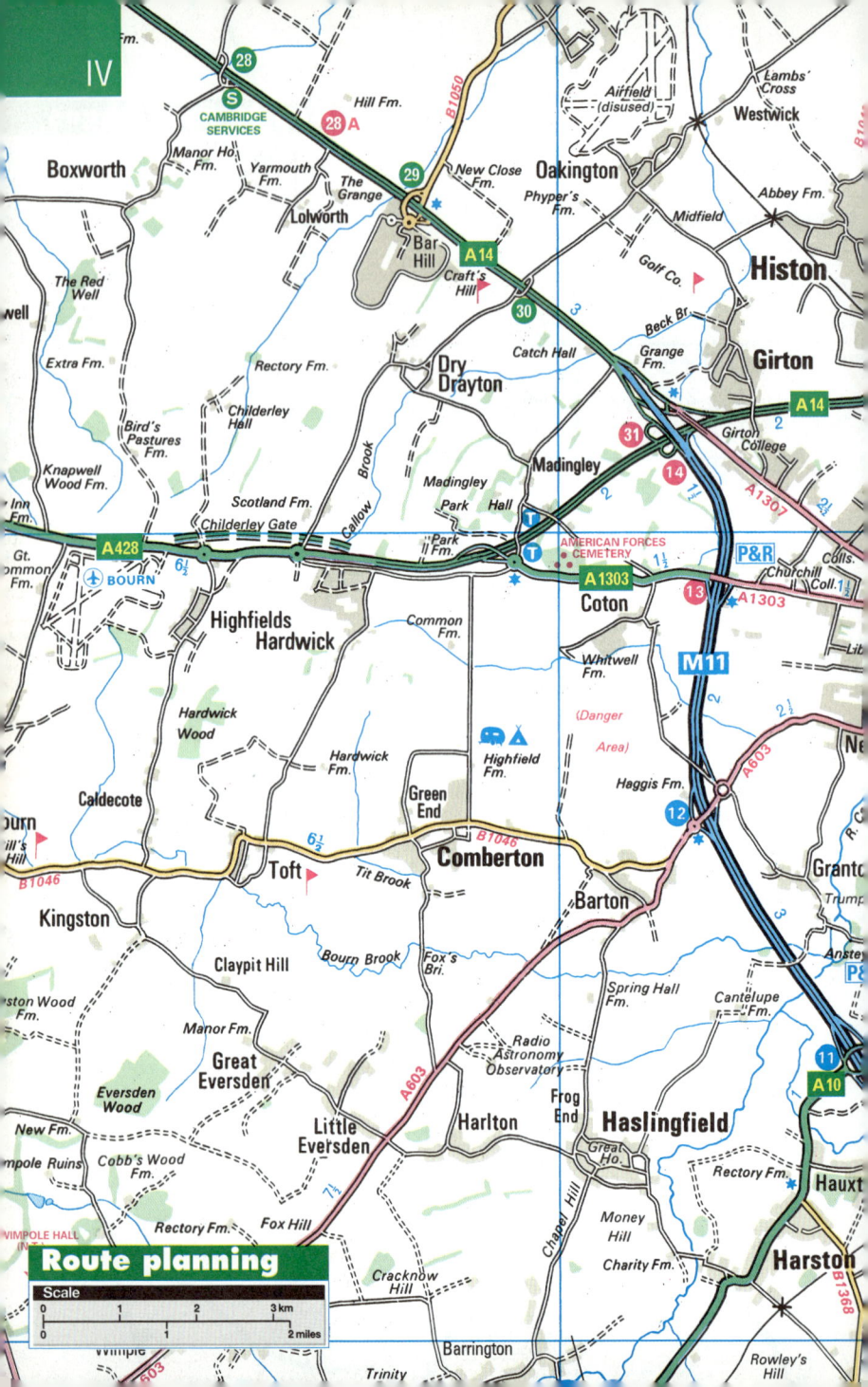

IV

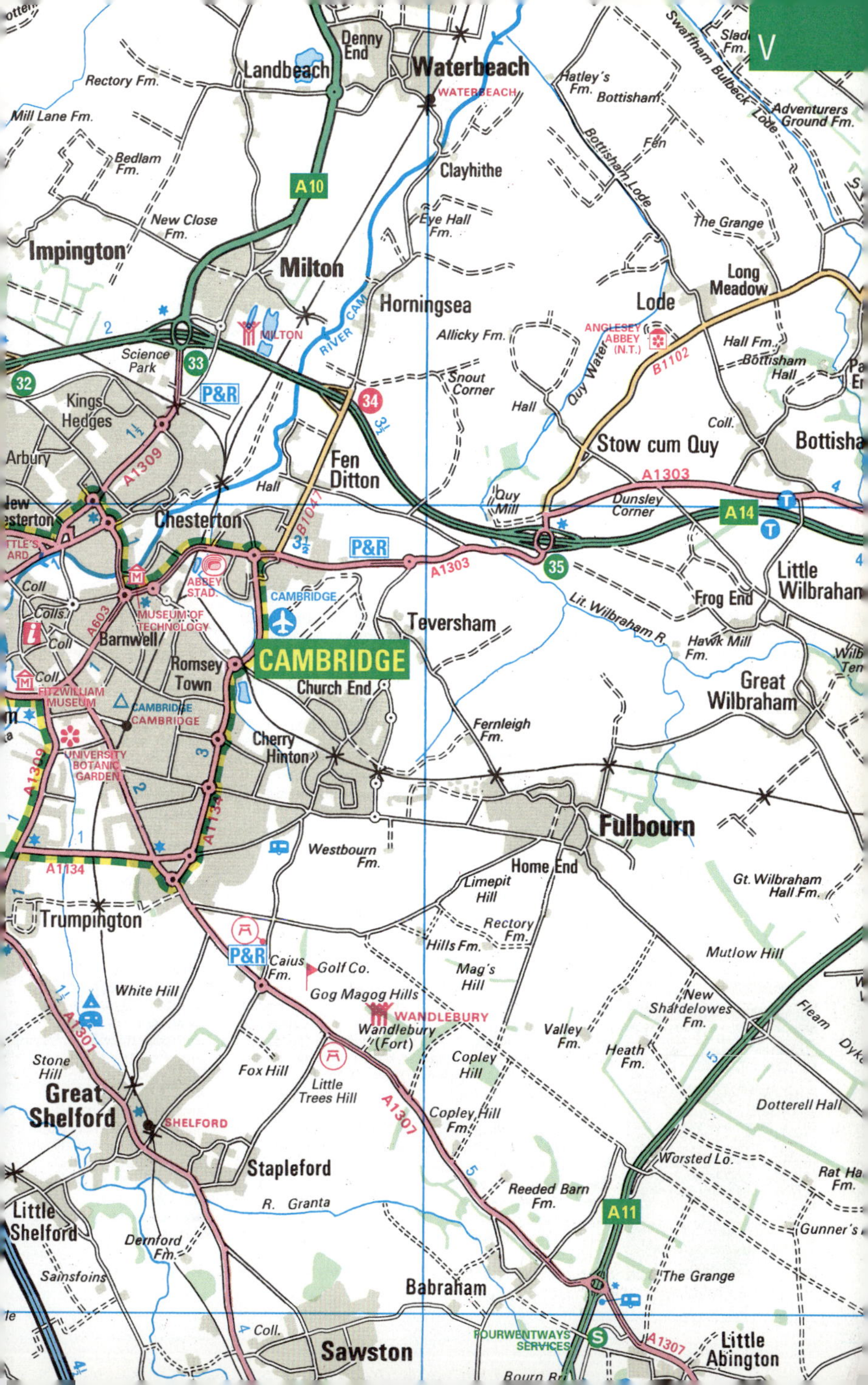
V
Denny End
Landbeach
Waterbeach
WATERBEACH
Rectory Fm.
Mill Lane Fm.
Hatley's Fm.
Bottisham
Swaffham Bulbeck Lode
Slade Fm.
Adventurers Ground Fm.
Bottisham Lode
Fen
Bedlam Fm.
Clayhithe
A10
New Close Fm.
Eye Hall Fm.
The Grange
Impington
Milton
Horningsea
Long Meadow
Lode
MILTON
RIVER CAM
Allicky Fm.
ANGLESEY ABBEY (N.T.)
Hall Fm.
Bottisham Hall
B1102
Science Park
33
32
P&R
Kings Hedges
Snout Corner
34
Quy Water
Hall
Coll.
Stow cum Quy
Bottisham
Arbury
A1309
Fen Ditton
Hall
A1303
Chesterton
B1047
Quy Mill
Dunsley Corner
A14
P&R
A1303
35
ABBEY STAD.
Little Wilbraham
Coll
Colls.
Coll
Coll
CAMBRIDGE
Lit. Wilbraham R.
Frog End
A603
MUSEUM OF TECHNOLOGY
Barnwell
Teversham
Hawk Mill Fm.
CAMBRIDGE
Romsey Town
Church End
Great Wilbraham
FITZWILLIAM MUSEUM
CAMBRIDGE
CAMBRIDGE
Fernleigh Fm.
UNIVERSITY BOTANIC GARDEN
Cherry Hinton
A1309
A1134
Fulbourn
Westbourn Fm.
A1134
Home End
Limepit Hill
Gt. Wilbraham Hall Fm.
Trumpington
Rectory Fm.
Hills Fm.
P&R
Caius Fm.
Golf Co.
Mutlow Hill
Mag's Hill
White Hill
Gog Magog Hills
WANDLEBURY
Wandlebury (Fort)
New Shardelowes Fm.
Fleam Dyke
A1301
Valley Fm.
Stone Hill
Fox Hill
Copley Hill
Heath Fm.
Little Trees Hill
A1307
Great Shelford
SHELFORD
Copley Hill Fm.
Dotterell Hall
Stapleford
Worsted Lo.
Rat Hall Fm.
R. Granta
Reeded Barn Fm.
A11
Little Shelford
Dernford Fm.
Gunner's
Sainsfoins
The Grange
Babraham
Coll.
FOURWENTWAYS SERVICES
Sawston
A1307
Little Abington
Bourn Br.

Sights of Cambridge

University

Christ's College *St Andrew's Street* founded 1505, though initially as God's-house in 1437, Christ's College moved to its present site in 1448 and finally, with a royal charter, re-founded as Christ's College in 1505. Beautiful gardens with limited opening hours. ☎01223 334900
🖥 www.christs.cam.ac.uk 44 B3

Churchill College *Storey's Way* founded 1960 Churchill College is the national and Commonwealth memorial to Sir Winston Churchill, best known as British Prime Minister during World War II.
☎01223 336000
🖥 www.chu.cam.ac.uk 17 A1

Clare College *Trinity Lane* founded 1326 Clare College is the second oldest of Cambridge's thirty-one colleges. Beautiful court and gardens. ☎01223 333200
🖥 www.clare.cam.ac.uk 45 A2

Clare Hall *Herschel Road* founded 1965 Clare Hall was founded by the Master and Fellows of Clare College and given the name by which the founding college had been known up to the mid 19th century. ☎01223 332360
🖥 www.clarehall.cam.ac.uk
25 A3

Corpus Christi *Trumpington Street* Founded 1352 Corpus was formed by townspeople, members of two Cambridge guilds - the Guild of Corpus Christi and the Guild of the Blessed Virgin Mary, primarily to train priests. ☎01223 338000
🖥 www.corpus.cam.ac.uk 45 A2

▼ *Christ's College*

Darwin College *Silver Street* founded 1964 as the first college in Cambridge exclusively for graduate students, on the initiative of Trinity, St John's, and Gonville and Caius Colleges. ☎01223 335660
🖥 www.dar.cam.ac.uk 45 A1

Downing College *Regent Street* founded 1800 by Sir George Downing with wealth left by his grandfather, who served both Cromwell and Charles II, and built No 10 Downing Street. ☎01223 334800
🖥 www.dow.cam.ac.uk 45 B1

Emmanuel College *St Andrew's Street* founded 1584 by Sir Walter Mildmay, Elizabeth I's Chancellor of the Exchequer. Christopher Wren designed the chapel in 1666, the façade with Corinthian columns, pediment and cupola. Beautiful gardens and many ducks, suitable feed for whom may be bought from the porter's lodge.
☎01223 334200
🖥 www.emma.cam.ac.uk 45 B2

Fitzwilliam College *Huntingdon Road* founded 1966 Fitzwilliam celebrated its 125th anniversary in the academic year 1994-95, having followed a direct line of development from a seed planted in the university in 1869. ☎01223 332000
🖥 www.fitz.cam.ac.uk 17 A2

Girton College *Huntingdon Road* founded in 1869 under the name of the College for Women in 1872 the college was renamed Girton College and moved to the current buildings in October 1873, receiving the status of a College of the University in 1948 when women were finally admitted to full membership of the university. ☎01223 338999
🖥 www.girton.cam.ac.uk 25 A4

Gonville and Caius College *Trinity Street* founded 1348 by Edmund Gonville, Rector of Terrington, then after a period of decline, refounded and extended in 1557 by former student and Fellow, Dr John Caius. Dr Caius had been living in Padua in Italy, where he studied and practised medicine. Whilst in Italy, he Latinised the spelling of his original surname Keys, to Caius, although it has always

▲ *Corpus Christi College*

been pronounced 'keys'. Beautiful Caius Court and three gates of 'Humility', 'Virtue' and 'Honour'. ☎01223 332400
🖥 www.cai.cam.ac.uk 45 B1

Homerton College *Hills Road* founded 1976, Homerton's roots are as a dissenting academy in 1695 in London, in 1894 moved to its present site in Cambridge. In 1976 Homerton became an Approved Society of the University of Cambridge it was then part of the Faculty of Education. In 2001 Homerton became a constituent college.
🖥 www.homerton.cam.ac.uk
☎01223 507111 33 C3

Hughes Hall *Mortimer Road* founded 1885 Hughes Hall is the oldest Graduate College in Cambridge. It was unique in specialising in the admission of women graduates at a time when the University itself still did not confer degrees on women.
🖥 www.hughes.cam.ac.uk
☎01223 334898 45 C2

Jesus College *Jesus Lane* founded 1496 on the site of the twelfth-century Benedictine nunnery of St Mary and St Radegund, which was suppressed to make way for the new college. The college originally consisted of buildings taken over from the nunnery. These buildings remain the core of the college to this day, hence the monastic and non-collegiate character.
🖥 www.jesus.cam.ac.uk
☎01223 339339 44 B3

King's College, *King's Parade* founded 1441 by Henry VI. The college's buildings were intended to be a magnificent display of the power of royal patronage with King's College

Chapel the focal point. One of the chapel's most striking features is the painting *Adoration of the Magi* by Rubens.
🖥 www.kings.cam.ac.uk
☎01223 331100 45 A2

Lucy Cavendish College *Lady Margaret Road* founded 1965 for the specific advancement of women's education. Lucy Cavendish Collegiate Society accepted its first undergraduates in October 1972 and finally in 1997 the college was granted a Royal Charter and became a fully self-governing college within the university.
🖥 www.lucy-cav.ac.uk
☎01223 332190 17 B1

Magdalene College *Magdalene Street* founded 1428 by the Lord Chancellor to Henry VIII, Magdalene was the last all-male college of the university. Women were finally admitted in 1988. Samuel Pepys bequeathed his diaries and library to the college in 1703 and they are housed in the Pepys Building. ☎01223 332100
🖥 www.magd.cam.ac.uk 44 A4

New Hall *Huntingdon Road* founded 1954 as the third foundation for women students at Cambridge University at a time when Cambridge had the lowest proportion of women undergraduates of any university in the UK.
🖥 www.newhall.cam.ac.uk
☎01223 762100 17 B1

Newnham College *Sidgwick Avenue* founded 1871 to promote academic excellence for women. The buildings are grouped round a beautiful garden. ☎01223 335700
🖥 www.newn.cam.ac.uk 25 B2

Pembroke College *Trumpington Street* founded 1347 by Marie de St Pol wife of the Earl of

Pembroke. The chapel was the first college chapel in Cambridge. ℡01223 338100
🖥 www.pem.cam.ac.uk 45 A2

Peterhouse *Trumpington Street* founded 1284 Hugh de Balsham, Bishop of Ely, set up a scholars' foundation at what is now St John's College, in 1284 this foundation moved south to a site beside St Peter's Church (now Little St Mary's Church) and Peterhouse was established. The only visible trace of the original buildings is in the walls of the dining hall at the rear of Old Court.
🖥 www.pet.cam.ac.uk
℡01223 338200 45 A1

Queen's College *Silver Street* founded 1448 by two queens: Margaret of Anjou, Henry VI's queen, and Elizabeth Woodville, Edward VI's queen. 15th-century brick courtyard next to Cloister Court, itself a superb example of Tudor architecture. The college also contains the famous Mathematical Bridge, built in 1904 to the same specifications as the original 1749 model. It is however a myth that the original stood without bolts. Unpredictable opening hours. ℡01223 335511
🖥 www.quns.cam.ac.uk 45 A2

Robinson College *Grange Road* founded in 1979 by Sir David Robinson, an entrepreneur and philanthropist for whom Cambridge was his home town, it is one of the larger and friendlier colleges.
🖥 www.robinson.cam.ac.uk
℡01223 339100 25 A3

St Catharine's College *Trumpington Street* founded 1473 by the then provost of neighbouring King's College. Original buildings were demolished in 17th century to be replaced by a classical redbrick court. The money ran out before the fourth side was completed, so the college court opens out onto Trumpington Road. St Catharine's emblem, the golden wheel, commemorates Catharine of Alexandria who was crucified on a wheel.
🖥 www.caths.cam.ac.uk
℡01223 338300 45 A2

St Edmund's College *Mount Pleasant* founded 1896 by the 15th Duke of Norfolk and Baron Anatole von Hügel it finally became a full college of the University in 1985. In 1987, the college established the Von Hügel Institute for interdisciplinary study of Christianity and Society. The college admits men and women of all faiths and none, and prides itself on being an ecumenical community. Daily worship in the college chapel is celebrated according to the Roman Catholic rite.
🖥 www.st-edmunds.cam.ac.uk
℡01223 336250 17 B1

St John's College *St John's Street* founded 1511 from the estate of Lady Margaret Beaufort, mother of King Henry VII. The exterior of the gatehouse on St John's Street is very decorative with marguerite daisies, a fox disappearing into its burrow and a statue of St John the Evangelist. A series of courtyards leads to the river and the Bridge of Sighs, built in 1831. ℡01223 338600
🖥 www.joh.cam.ac.uk 44 B3

Selwyn College *Grange Road* founded 1882 to commemorate the life of George Augustus Selwyn, the first Anglican Bishop of New Zealand. Since then, it has maintained a close connection with the Anglican church. ℡01223 335846
🖥 www.sel.cam.ac.uk 25 A2

Senate House *Off King's Parade* 18th-century ceremonial centre of the university. Not open to the public. 45 A2

Sidney Sussex College *Sidney Street* founded 1596, on the eastern side is the chapel with its oak panelling, unmarked in the ante-chapel is Oliver Cromwell's head. A former student of Sidney Sussex he went on to lead the Parliamentarians to victory in the English Civil War. Upon the restoration of the monarchy, his body was exhumed and decapitated, the head put on display as a warning to traitors of the realm. Unpredictable opening hours. ℡01223 338800
🖥 www.sid.cam.ac.uk 44 B3

Trinity College *Trinity Street* founded 1546 by Henry VIII in the merging two existing colleges, Trinity is the wealthiest college in Cambridge, it is said that once one could walk from Cambridge to Oxford crossing only Trinity land. Famously, the Great Court is the setting for a scene in Chariots of Fire. ℡01223 338400
🖥 www.trin.cam.ac.uk 44 A3

Trinity Hall *Trinity Lane* Founded in 1350 by the Bishop of Norwich, the college was originally intended for the study of law. The pretty gardens, with their colourful flowerbeds, stretch all the way to the riverside.
🖥 www.trinhall.cam.ac.uk
℡01223 332500 45 A2

Wolfson College *Barton Road* founded 1965 it was called University College, but in 1972 the name was changed to Wolfson College following a generous donation from the Wolfson Foundation. The most cosmopolitan of the colleges with students and fellows from all over the world.
🖥 www.wolfson.cam.ac.uk
℡01223 335900 25 A2

Gardens, Parks and Nature Reserves

The Backs area along the back of the riverside colleges with daffodils and crocuses in the spring and stunning views across the river. 25 B4

Castle Mound grassy motte of William the Conqueror's castle. 44 A4

Christ's Pieces *Emmanuel Road* Victorian park with tree lined avenues, formal seasonal bedding displays, large ornamental shrub beds, Diana, Princess of Wales, Rose Garden, tennis

King's College and the River Cam

▲ *Cambridge City Centre*

courts, bowling green and small play area. 📞 01223 457532 44 B3

Fulborn Nature Reserve
A member of the Wildlife Trust and designated a Site of Special Scientific Interest. Nature reserve shown on mapping half a mile to the east of Fulborn 🌐 www.wildlifebcnp.org 📞 01223 712400 37 C2

Jesus Green *Chesterton Road*
Lock-keeper's garden, acres of grass, an avenue of plane trees, and an outdoor swimming pool in the summer. 📞 01223 457532 44 B4

Lammas Land A popular park with large play area and summer paddling pool. The area has many ancient willows. 45 A1

Milton Country Park
Cambridge Road, Milton
90 acres of parkland with wooded areas and lakes, including a visitor centre and picnic area. 🌐 www.scambs.gov.uk 📞 01223 420060 12 C3

The Orchard Tea Gardens
Mill Way, Grantchester
Attractive tea gardens also host to the Rupert Brooke Museum. 📞 01223 845788 31 C1

University Botanic Garden
Bateman Street Forty acres of gardens with lake, glasshouses and nine National Collections including geraniums. 🌐 www.botanic.cam.ac.uk 📞 01223 336265 26 A1

Wandlebury Country Park and Nature Reserve
On the site of an Iron-Age fort, features woodland, walks and a nature trail. 🌐 www.cpswandlebury.org 📞 01223 248706 41 C1

Places of Worship

Great St Mary, *Market Square*
Great St Mary's overlooks the market place. Building began in 1478 with the donation by Henry VII of 100 oak trees for the construction of the roof. The upper galleries were added in the 18th century, with 123 steps leading to the top of the bell tower, offering an excellent view of the city. www.ely.anglican.org/parishes/camgsm 45 A2

Church of the Holy Sepulchre (The Round Church), *Bridge Street* The distinctive round shape of this church originated in the Holy Land, where early Christians built circular walls around tombs. English crusaders returned from Palestine with a vivid memory of the design and the Round Church was built circa 1130. Altered in the 15th century with the addition of windows, and again in 1841. Today the Round Church houses the Brass Rubbing Centre. Tours of the church are free. 📞 01223 311602 44 A3

King's College Chapel *King's Parade* Built in three phases between 1446 and 1515, roughly according to the wishes of Henry VI, its founder. The chapel includes fan vaulting, 16th-century stained glass windows, choir screen and stalls which probably date to 1530s. The altarpiece is Rubens' Adoration of the Magi. 📞 01223 331212 🌐 www.kings.cam.ac.uk 45 A2

Little St Mary's *Little St Mary's Lane* The site of Little St Mary's Church was originally the home of St Peter's Church, which lives on in the name of the neighbouring college, Peterhouse. Whitewashed walls, long windows and painted roof beams. There is also a monument to the former vicar of the parish, Godfrey Washington, who was the great uncle of the first US president, George Washington. The family coat-of-arms, a black eagle on a shield of red stars and stripes is said to be the origin of the US flag. 🌐 www.ely.anglican.org/parishes/camlsm 📞 01223 366202 45 A2

The Church of Our Lady & the English Martyrs *Hills Road* The building of the church was financed by Yolande Marie Louise Lyne-Stevens, a celebrated ballerina. Construction was completed in 1890, the result being a neo-Gothic design with a 214 foot (65.2 m) spire. The church is decorated with stained-glass windows and murals, many of the English Christian martyrs. There is also a 16th-century wooden statue of the Virgin Mary. 🌐 www.olem.org.uk 📞 01223 350787 45 C1

St Andrew the Great *St Andrew's Street* built in 1843, on the site where an older church had burnt down, it contains a memorial to Captain James Cook, the English navigator. His wife is buried in the nave as are two of his sons. 📞 01223 518219 45 B2

St Bene't *Benet Street* St Bene't's (St Benedict's) Church predates the Norman conquest of England in 1066, and so the church stood long before the establishment of the university. The Anglo-Saxon tower remains. Inside there are colourful angels on the roof beams of the north transept, an arch and pair of lions dating from around 1000. Change-ringing (ringing bells to a tune), was first developed on these bells by Fabian Stedman. Call prior to visit for disabled access arrangements. 📞 01223 353903 www.stbenets.com 45 A2

St Botolph's Church *Trumpington Street* St Botolph was the patron saint of travellers in medieval times churches dedicated to him often sited at the entrance to a town. St Botolph's Church was built around 1320. Its 15th-century tower is topped with symbols of the four Evangelists: the man, the eagle, the ox and the lion. On its walls are two sundials and a clock. Painted roof and 17th-century font. 📞 01223 363529 45 A1

St Edward's Church *Peas Hill*
Dedicated to Edward the Confessor, the church is a mixture of styles with a 12th-century tower, 14th-century arches and a 15th-century chancel. Two side aisles were added to serve as chapels to Clare College and Trinity Hall. Most of the windows are a later addition. 📞 01223 362004 🌐 www.st-edwards-cam.org.uk 45 A2

St John's College Chapel
St John's Street Gothic revival, built in 1860s - with bits of original late 12th-century chapel – by Sir George Gilbert Scott. Includes Victorian stained glass and some 16th-century monuments. 📞 01223 338600 🌐 www.joh.cam.ac.uk/chapel_and_choir 44 A3

St Michael *Trinity Street*
St Michael's Church was built in the mid-14th century and originally served as the college chapel of Michaelhouse. Much of the original decorated gothic design remains. In 1908, the parish was amalgamated into

▼ *American Military Cemetery*

that of Great St Mary's, and the church is now used for book sales and meetings. It also houses the Harambee Centre, which promotes education and understanding about underdeveloped countries.
🖥 www.michaelhouse.org.uk
📞 01223 309167 44 A3

St Mary and St Michael Grantchester Road, Trumpington
An elegant church with a brass of Sir Roger de Trumpington (1289), the second oldest in England. 📞 01223 841262 38 B4

Museums and Galleries

American Military Cemetery Coton Road, Madingley Thirty-acre site donated by the University of Cambridge. 3,812 American military dead buried there. The wall from the entrance to the chapel bears the inscription of names of the 5,126 Americans who died serving their country, but whose remains were never recovered or identified.
🖥 www.abmc.gov/ca.htm
📞 01954 210350 14 C2

Cambridge and County Folk Museum Castle Street The heritage and history of Cambridge from 17th century to today.
🖥 www.folkmuseum.org.uk
📞 01223 355159 44 A4

Cambridge Museum of Technology Cheddars Lane
Victorian pumping station and working museum with the status of industrial national monument. 📞 01223 368650
🖥 www.museumoftechnology.com 19 A1

The Fitzwilliam Museum Trumpington Street Egyptian, Greek, Roman and western Asiatic antiquities, vast range of European arts, manuscripts, armour, sculpture, furniture, pottery, coins, medals.
🖥 www.fitzmuseum.cam.ac.uk
📞 01223 332900 45 A1

Kettle's Yard Castle Street 20th-century art, including Barbara Hepworth and Ben Nicholson; music, with a series of professional chamber music concerts held in the house during university terms, student lunch-time recitals, concerts of new music and collaborations with Cambridge Modern Jazz Club and Jazz East. 📞 01223 352124
🖥 www.kettlesyard.co.uk 44 A4

Rupert Brooke Museum Mill Way, Grantchester 📞 01223 845788
🖥 www.rupertbrooke.com 31 C1

Scott Polar Research Institute Lensfield Road Contains relics of Sir Robert Scott's journey to the Antarctic as well as those of other polar explorers. Also displays of Lapp and Eskimo life and polar wildlife.
📞 01223 336540 45 B1
🖥 www.spri.cam.ac.uk

The Sedgwick Museum of Earth Sciences Downing Street
Extensive collection of fossils, rocks and minerals from around the world. 📞 01223 333456 45 B2
🖥 www.sedgwickmuseum.org

University Library West Road
Regular exhibitions.
🖥 www.lib.cam.ac.uk
📞 01223 333000 25 B3

University Museum of Archaeology and Anthropology Downing Street Illustrates prehistoric and recent traditional cultures from all parts of the world, also local archaeology.
📞 01223 333516
🖥 http://museum-server.archanth.cam.ac.uk/ 45 B2

University Museum of Classical Archaeology, Sidgwick Avenue
Plaster casts of Greek and Roman sculptures.
📞 01223 335153 🖥 www.classics.cam.ac.uk/ark.html 25 B2

University Museum of Zoology, Downing Street Contains material collected by Charles Darwin. Various zoological exhibits, including reconstruction of a rocky shore with bird life, an extinct giant ground sloth and a giant spider crab.
📞 01223 336650
🖥 www.zoo.cam.ac.uk 45 B2

Whipple Museum of the History of Science Free School Lane
A comprehensive collection of scientific instruments and models, used by staff and students of the university for research.
🖥 www.hps.cam.ac.uk/whipple
📞 01223 330906 45 A2

Entertainment

ADC Theatre Park Street
📞 01223 5033333 44 A3
🖥 www.adc-theatre.cam.ac.uk

Arts Picture House St Andrews Street 📞 01223 504444 45 B2
🖥 www.picturehouses.co.uk

Cambridge Arts Theatre St Edwards Passage
📞 01223 503333 45 A2 🖥 www.cambridgeartstheatre.com

Cineworld Cambridge Leisure Park, Clifton Way 📞 0871 2208000 33 C4
🖥 www.cineworld.co.uk

The Junction Clifton Road
📞 01223 511511 33 C4
🖥 www.junction.co.uk

Mumford Theatre East Road 📞 01223 352932 45 C2
🖥 www.apu.ac.uk/mumfordtheatre

Vue Grafton Centre 📞 08712 240240
🖥 www.myvue.com 44 C3

Pubs

The Anchor Silver Street
📞 01223 353554 45 A1

The Baron of Beef Bridge Street
📞 01223 505022 44 A3

The Champion of the Thames King Street 📞 01223 352043 44 B3

The Maypole Portugal Place
📞 01223 352999 44 A3

The Mill Mill Lane
📞 01223 357026 45 A2

The Mitre Tavern Bridge Street
📞 01223 358403 44 A3

Activities

Cycle Hire

H Drake 56-60 Hills Road
📞 01223 363468 45 C1

The Bikeman Cambridge Market Square
🖥 www.thebikeman.co.uk
📞 0785 0814186 45 A2

Cambridge Station Cycles Station Building, Station Road
🖥 www.stationcycles.co.uk
📞 01223 307125 26 C1

City Cycle Hire 61 Newnham Road
🖥 www.citycyclehire.com
📞 01223 365629 25 B2

Mike's Bikes 28 Mill Road
📞 01223 312591 45 B2

NYK Bike Hire 210 Cherry Hinton Road 📞 01223 505485 34 A4

University Cycles 9 Victoria Avenue
📞 01223 355517 44 B3

Punting

Cambridge Chauffeur Punts Silver Street 📞 01223 354164
🖥 www.punting-in-cambridge.co.uk 45 A1

Scudamores Punting Company Granta Place, Mill Lane
🖥 www.scudamores.com
📞 01223 359750 45 A2

The Granta Punting Company Newnham Road
🖥 www.puntingincambridge.com 📞 01223 301845 25 B2

Trinity Punts, Garret Hostel Bridge
📞 01223 338483
🖥 www.trin.cam.ac.uk 44 A3

Other Activities

Aeromega Helicopters Cambridge Airport, Newmarket Road
🖥 www.aeromega.com
📞 01223 294488 20 B1

Cambridge United Football Club, The Abbey Stadium, Newmarket Road 🖥 www.cambridge-united.premiumtv.co.uk
📞 01223 56650019 B1

Cambridge University Cricket Club Fenner's, Mortimer Road
🖥 www.srcf.ucam.org/cucc
📞 01223 353552 45 C1

Cambridge University Rugby Union Football Ground 📞 University Football Ground 01223 354131
🖥 www.curufc.com 24 C1

Girton Golf Club Dodford Lane, Girton 📞 01223 276169 9 A4

Gog Magog Golf Club Babraham Road 📞 01223 246058 41 A3

Laser Quest Bradwells Court
🖥 www.laserquest.co.uk
📞 01223 302102 45 B2

Megabowl Cambridge Leisure, Clifton Way 📞 0871 5501010
🖥 www.tenpin.co.uk 33 C4

Information

Tourist Information The Old Library, Wheeler Street
🖥 www.visitcambridge.org
📞 0906 5862526 45 A2

Cambridge City Council
📞 01223 457000
🖥 www.cambridge.gov.uk

Traveline – impartial public transport information
📞 0870 6082608
🖥 www.traveline.org.uk

National Rail 📞 08457 484950
🖥 www.nationalrail.co.uk

One 📞 0845 6007245
🖥 www.onerailway.com

Wagn 📞 0870 8508822
🖥 www.wagn.co.uk

Stagecoach 🖥 www.stagecoachbus.com/cambridge

Huntingdon and District Bus Service 📞 01480 453159
🖥 www.huntsbus.co.uk

Whippet Coaches Ltd
📞 01480 463792
🖥 www.go-whippet.co.uk

Cambridge City Car Parks
📞 01223 458500

National Car Parks
🖥 www.ncp.co.uk

Stansted Airport
📞 0870 0000303
www.baa.co.ukmain/airports/stansted

2

Oakington

CB4

- Longstanton Road
- Manor Farm Cl
- Church Vw
- Mill Rd
- Station Road
- Vicarage Cl
- Meadow Farm Cl
- High Street
- Queens Wy
- Water Lane
- Lowbury Cr
- Coles La
- Longstanton Rd
- Croft La
- The Drift
- Mead View
- Cherry Or
- Holme Cl
- Arcadia Gd
- Arcadia Gd
- Oakington CE Prim Sch
- Whitehall Farm
- Kettles Cl
- Phypers Farm
- Oakington Farm
- The Broadway
- Orchard Wy
- Mansel Farm
- Fare Acres Farm
- Cambridge Road
- Dry Drayton Road
- Midfield
- Poplar Farm
- Mast

PO — Post Office
PH — Public House
LC — Level Crossing

Westwick
Westwick Hall

Unwins Farm

BARROW CROFTS
ALSTEAD RD
COTTE
CROFT CL
CLAY S
WINDERS
ST ANDREW'S PK
NUN
Abbey Farm
CHURCH ST
Histon Manor
Moat
WINDMILL
CASE WY
PARK LANE
BELLHILL
Girton LC
MELVIN WY
PARK LANE
HARDING
SCHOOL H
PARK LANE
ST AUDREY'S CL
MANOR PARK
AINGERS RD
PARK AVENUE
SHIRLEY RD
MERTON RD
MANOR PK
SOMERSET ROAD
HOME CLOSE
SA
n Acre arm
OAKINGTON ROAD
NEW SCH
Factory
Girton Farm
Park Farm
Histon & Impington Inf Sch
MANOR FARM RD
(dis)
OAK
FAIRWAY
Manor Farm
NORTHFIE

Moor
Farm
A
B
C
65
4
3
64
2
1
62
COTTENHAM ROAD
Unwins
Farm
COTTENHAM ROAD
BARROW-
CROFTS
CROFT
CL
CLAY
ST
ALSTEAD RD
GREENLEAS
NORMANTON
WY
FARMSTEAD
CL
PARLOUR CL
BURKETT WY
MUNCEY
WK
GARDEN
WK
CB4
YOUNGMAN CL
YOUNGMAN
AVE
MILL LANE
ST ANDREW'S
PK
WINDERS
LANE
CLAY
STREET
OLD
FARM CL
NUN'S
OR
LUCKETTS
CL
LANE
B1049
ORCHARD
ROAD
DRAKE
WAY
Abbey
Farm
3
CHURCH ST
SYMONDS
CL
NARROW
GLEBE
WAY
SPRING CL
PADDOCK CL
Histon
Manor
Moat
BELLHILL
WINDMILL
LA
PRIOR'S CL
Histon &
Impington
Jun Sch
Cemy
AMBROSE
WAY
PARK LANE
HILL
SCHOOL
MANOR
PARK
HARDING WY
Liby
PO
HIGH ST
ST AUDREY'S CL
PARK
AVENUE
AINGERS
RD
SHIRLEY RD
MERTON RD
HOME CLOSE
DWYER-JOYCE CL
STATION
ROAD
BROOK CL
Histon
PH
MANOR PK
SOMERSET ROAD
WEST
RD
WATER
LANE
IMPINGTON
LANE
HEREWARD CL
BISHOP
WAY
HEREWARD
CLOSE
CLAY
CLOSE
LANE
BURGOYNES
FARM CL
ROAD
SAFFRON ROAD
ROSELEA
BURGOYNE'S
DOCTOR
CL
Factory
NEW SCHOOL RD
NEW SCHOOL RD
THE DOLE
HOMEFIELD
CL
THE DOLE
NEW
ROAD
Sports
Ctr
PERCHERON
CL
Park
Farm
Histon &
Impington
Inf Sch
POPLAR
RD
STATION
HENRY MORRIS
RD
3
2
1
4
Impington
Village Coll
OAK TREE WAY
PARK DR
LOVE'S
CL
KAY HITCH
WAY
MACFARLANE
CL
1 BRACKENBURY CL
2 DAVEY CL
3 PARR CL
4 SCHOOL LA
(dis)
CHEQUERS
RD
CHIVERS
WAY
44
10
BRIDGE
ROAD
MOWLAM
CL
PO
Impington

Lane
arm

Oldfield Farm

Old Field Farm

Bedlam Farm

Manor Farm

MILTON ROAD

ST ANDREWS WAY

ST GEORGES WY

Green Gates Farm

Middlewhite Farm

Mereway Farm

Sun Close Farm

New Close Farm

BUTT LANE

6

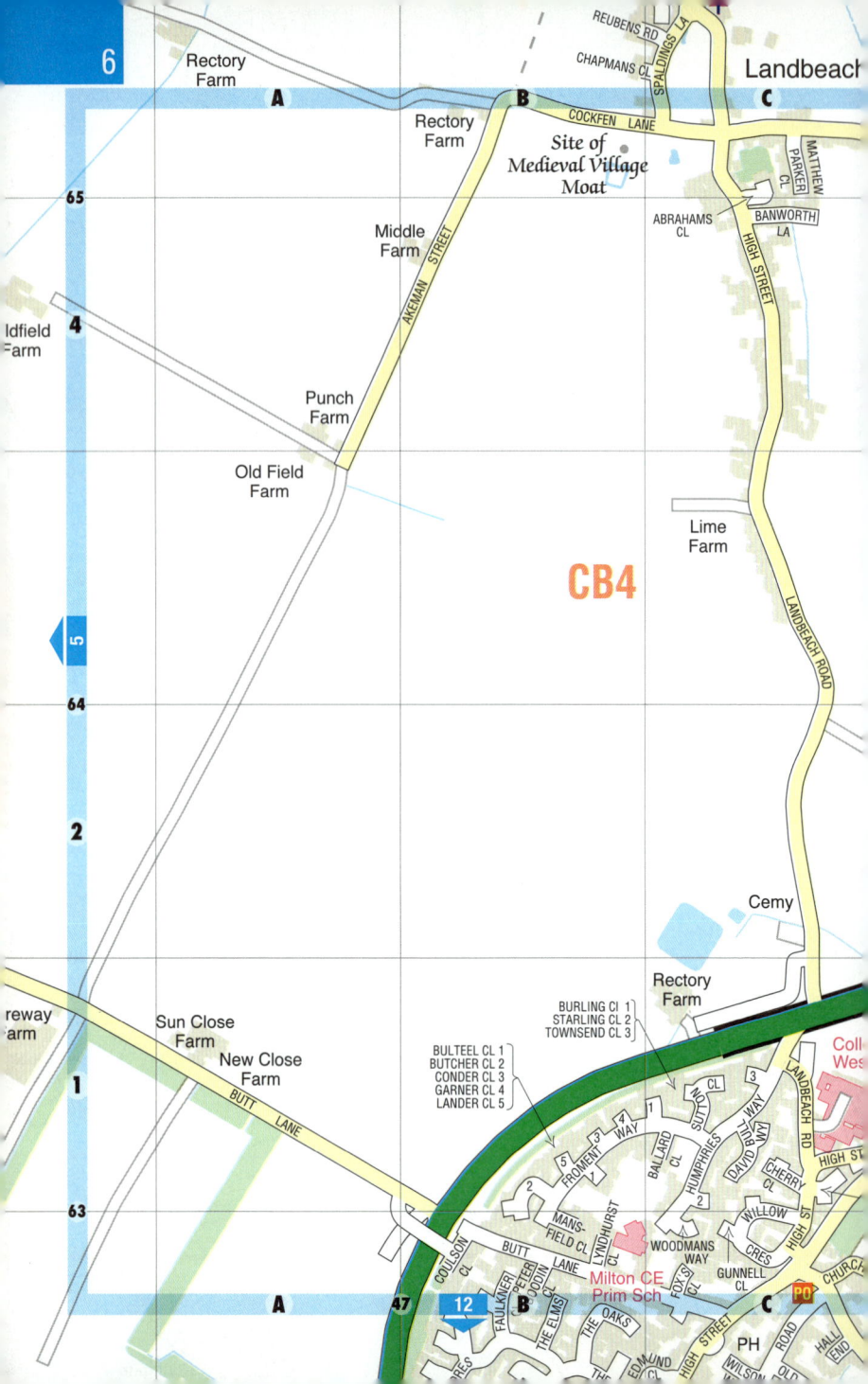

Landbeach

REUBENS RD
CHAPMANS CL
SPALDINGS LA
COCKFEN LANE
Rectory Farm
Rectory Farm
Site of Medieval Village Moat
MATTHEW PARKER CL
ABRAHAMS CL
BANWORTH LA
HIGH STREET
Middle Farm
AKEMAN STREET
Idfield Farm
Punch Farm
Old Field Farm
Lime Farm
LANDBEACH ROAD

CB4

Cemy

Rectory Farm

BURLING CL 1
STARLING CL 2
TOWNSEND CL 3

BULTEEL CL 1
BUTCHER CL 2
CONDER CL 3
GARNER CL 4
LANDER CL 5

reway arm
Sun Close Farm
New Close Farm
BUTT LANE
COLLSON CL
FAULKNER
PETER ODIN
BUTT LANE
THE ELMS
MANSFIELD CL
FROMENT
LYNDHURST
WOODMANS WAY
BALLARD CL
HUMPHRIES
SULLY CL
DAVID BULL WAY
CHERRY CL
WILLOW CRES
GUNNELL CL
Milton CE Prim Sch
LANDBEACH RD
HIGH ST
Coll West
CHURCH
HIGH STREET
WILSON
HALL RD
PH
THE OAKS
EDMUND

A10 Ely
Sandal Wood
CAMBRIDGE RD
PH
CAR DYKE RD   CAR DYKE ROAD
WATERBEACH ROAD
GLEBE ROAD
MILL RD
GIBSON CL
CORONATION CL
CAMBRIDGE ROAD
CHAPEL
STATION
ST JOHN'S CL
WHITM

CB5

The Hawks
Hall Farm
Hepworth Farm
ELY ROAD
River Cam

Stanton Farm
A10
Penfold Farm

CB4

Roman Pottery Kilns (site of)
CLAYHITHE ROAD

ELY ROAD

Milton
Fen Farm
13   49
Manor Farm
DOCK LANE
ST JOHN
Northgate

7
A B C
65
4
3
64
2
1
63
A B C

8

CB3

A14 Huntingdon

Catch Hall

Brook Farm

THE AVENUE

Hanchard Plantation

Grange Farm

M11

WASHPIT ROAD

WOODLANDS CL

LAWRENCE CL

Mast

A14

A428

14

M11

Biotechnology Centre

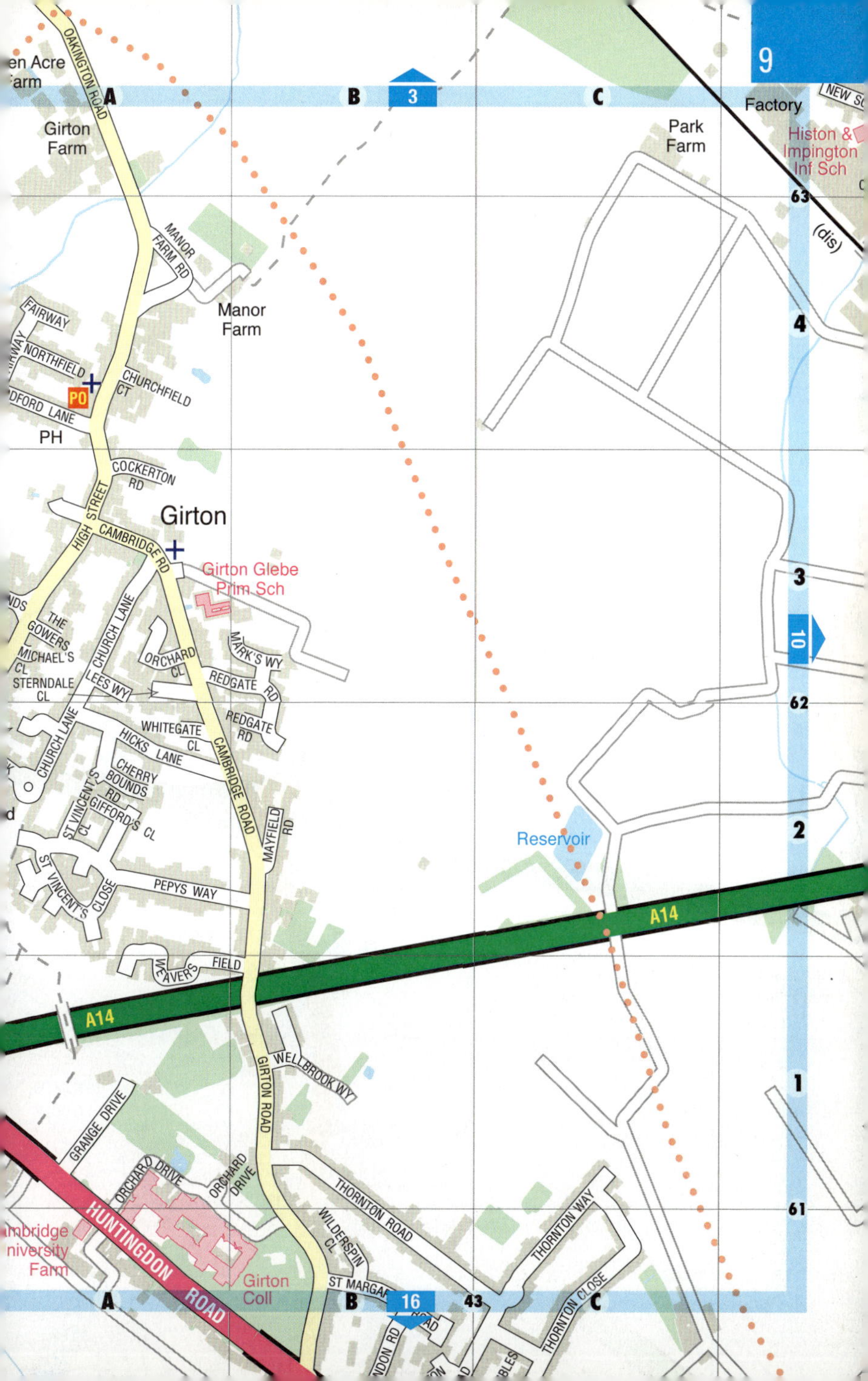
en Acre
Farm
Girton
Farm
OAKINGTON ROAD
A
B
3
C
Factory
NEW S
Park
Farm
Histon &
Impington
Inf Sch
63
(dis)
MANOR
FARM RD
Manor
Farm
4
FAIRWAY
NORTHFIELD
CHURCHFIELD
CT
CHURCHFIELD
PO
DFORD LANE
PH
COCKERTON
RD
HIGH STREET
Girton
CAMBRIDGE RD
Girton Glebe
Prim Sch
3
10
THE
GOWERS
MICHAEL'S
CL
STERNDALE
CL
CHURCH LANE
LEES WY
ORCHARD
CL
MARK'S WY
REDGATE
RD
REDGATE
RD
62
WHITEGATE
CL
HICKS LANE
CHERRY
BOUNDS
RD
CAMBRIDGE ROAD
ST VINCENT'S
CL
GIFFORD'S CL
MAYFIELD
RD
Reservoir
2
ST VINCENT'S CLOSE
PEPYS WAY
A14
WEAVERS FIELD
A14
WELLBROOK WY
GIRTON ROAD
1
GRANGE DRIVE
ORCHARD DRIVE
ORCHARD
DRIVE
THORNTON ROAD
WILDERSPIN
CL
THORNTON WAY
61
HUNTINGDON
ROAD
mbridge
niversity
Farm
Girton
Coll
ST MARGA
A
B
16
43
C
THORNTON CLOSE

10

Park Farm

Factory

Histon & Impington Inf Sch

SAFFRON ROAD
SCHOOL RD
BISHOP WAY
HERNARD CL
HEWARD CL
BURGOYNES FARM CL
CLAY
ROAD
DOCTOR CL
NEW SCHOOL RD
POPLAR RD
STATION RD
CLOSE
ROSELEA
HOMEFIELD
NEW ROAD
BURGOYNES CL
PERCHERON CL

Oak Tree Way
THE DOLE
HENRY MORRIS RD
THE DOLE

Sports Ctr

Impington Village Coll

LOVE'S CL
KAY HITCH WAY
CHEQUERS RD
CHIVERS WAY
McFARLANE
PARK DR

1 BRACKENBURY CL
2 DAVEY CL
3 PARR CL
4 SCHOOL LA

(dis)

BRIDGE ROAD

MOWLAM CL

Impington

PO

Histon Football Club

SOUTH ROAD
VILLA RD
VILLA PL
NEW RD
PEPYS TR
COLLEGE RD
THE CRES
CRESCENT ROAD
CAMBRIDGE RD
BURRO
Windmill

Millfield Farm

MILL RD
HIGHFIELD RD
THE COPPICE
B1049
BRIDGE RD

Hotel

CAMBRIDGE ROAD
BRIDGE RD
B1049

LONE TREE AVE
LONE TREE GROVE

A14

Impington Farm

CAMBRIDGE ROAD
B1049

C1
1 CRISPIN CL
2 SUNSET SQ
3 PLUM TREE CL
4 AYLESBOROUGH CL
5 WHITE ROSE WK
6 STURMER CL

CB4

HOWGATE RD
ELLISON CL
KING
CALLAN
St Laure RC Prim

ST CATHARINES SQ
ST CATHARINES RD
DAISY CL
Rec Gnd

BLACKHALL ROAD
WALNUT TREE WY
SUNFLOWER CL
ST ALBANS RD
VERULAM

BRIERLEY WAY
BLANDFORD WK
HAZELWOOD CLOSE
JERMIN

BROWNLOW
PELHAM CL
MOL
WOOD CL
MOLEWOOD

Arbury
C4
1 FORDWICH CL
2 NORTHUMBERLAND CL
3 BRACKLEY CL
ROSEFORD ROAD
RUTLAND CL
VERULA

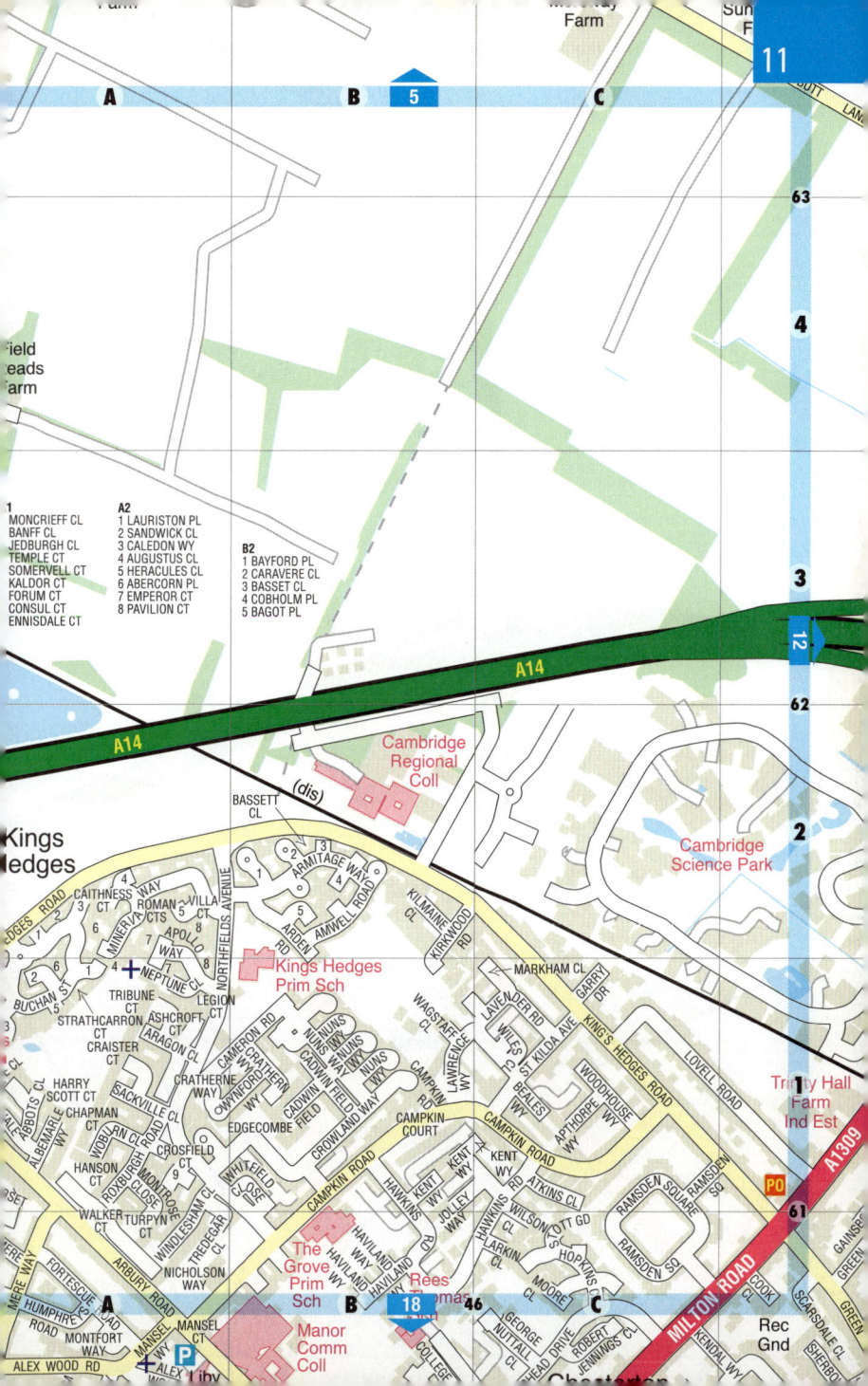

1
MONCRIEFF CL
BANFF CL
JEDBURGH CL
TEMPLE CT
SOMERVELL CT
KALDOR CT
FORUM CT
CONSUL CT
ENNISDALE CT

A2
1 LAURISTON PL
2 SANDWICK CL
3 CALEDON WY
4 AUGUSTUS CL
5 HERACULES CL
6 ABERCORN PL
7 EMPEROR CT
8 PAVILION CT

B2
1 BAYFORD PL
2 CARAVERE CL
3 BASSET CL
4 COBHOLM PL
5 BAGOT PL

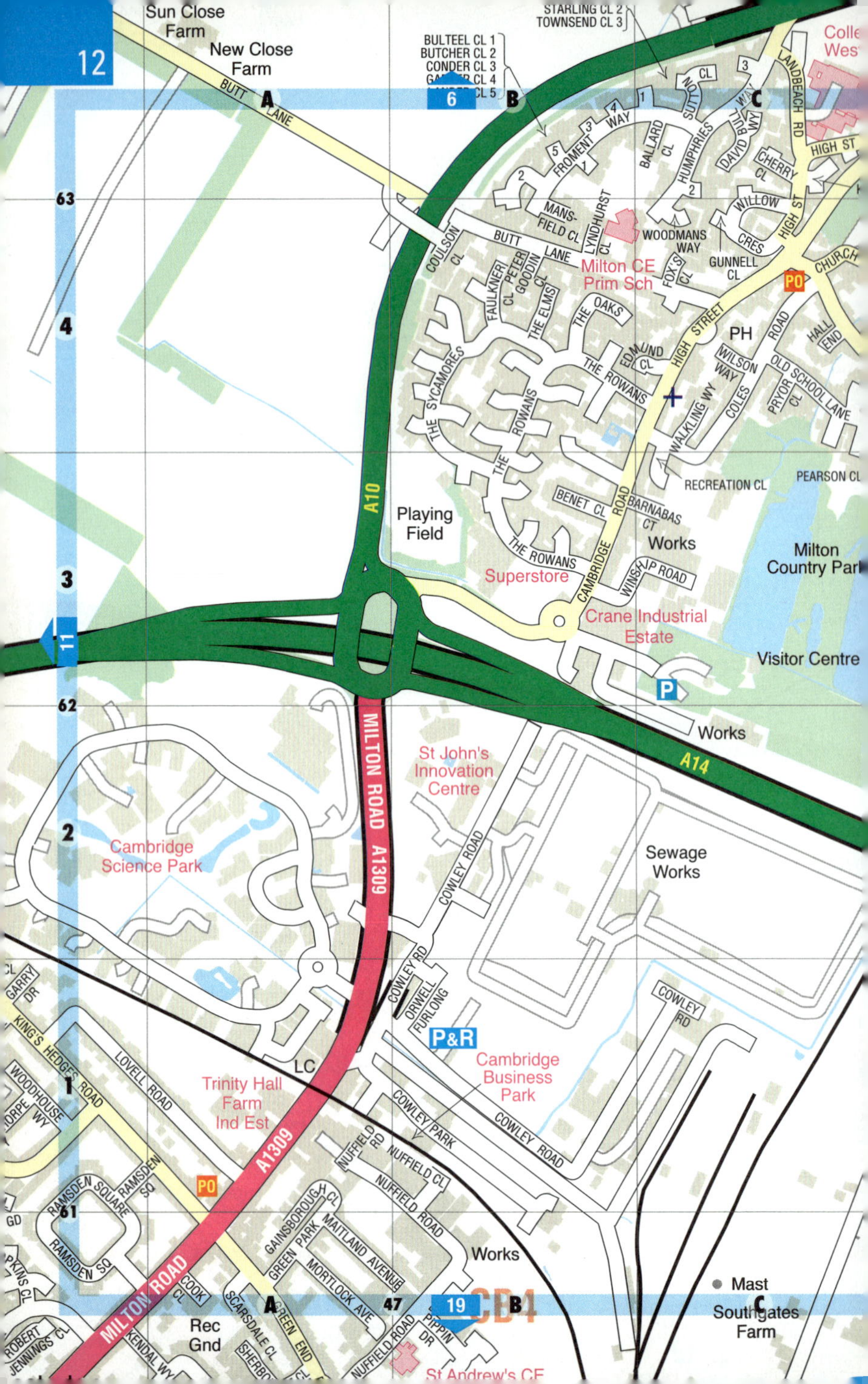
Sun Close Farm
New Close Farm
BUTT LANE
STARLING CL 2
TOWNSEND CL 3
BULTEEL CL 1
BUTCHER CL 2
CONDER CL 3
CL 4
CL 5
6
A
B
C
Colle
Wes
LANDBEACH RD
HIGH ST
WAY
FROMENT
SUTTON CL
BALLARD CL
HUMPHRIES WAY
DAVID BULL WY
CHERRY CL
WILLOW CRES
MANS-FIELD CL
LYNDHURST CL
WOODMANS WAY
GUNNELL CL
COULSON CL
BUTT LANE
Milton CE Prim Sch
FOX'S CL
HIGH ST
CHURCH
PO
FAULKNER CL
PETER GOODIN CL
THE ELMS
THE OAKS
HIGH STREET
PH
ROAD
HALL END
WILSON WAY
OLD SCHOOL LANE
PRYOR CL
COLES
WALKLING WY
EDMUND CL
THE ROWANS
THE SYCAMORES
THE ROWANS
THE
RECREATION CL
PEARSON CL
63
4
A10
Playing Field
BENET CL
BARNABAS CT
CAMBRIDGE ROAD
Works
Milton Country Park
THE ROWANS
Superstore
WINSHIP ROAD
3
Crane Industrial Estate
Visitor Centre
11
P
62
Works
A14
MILTON ROAD
A1309
St John's Innovation Centre
COWLEY ROAD
2
Cambridge Science Park
Sewage Works
CL
GARRY DR
COWLEY RD
ORWELL FURLONG
COWLEY RD
P&R
KING'S HEDGES ROAD
LOVELL ROAD
WOODHOUSE WY
ORPE
1
LC
Trinity Hall Farm Ind Est
Cambridge Business Park
COWLEY PARK
COWLEY ROAD
A1309
NUFFIELD RD
NUFFIELD CL
NUFFIELD ROAD
RAMSDEN SQUARE
RAMSDEN SQ
PO
61
GD
RAMSDEN SQ
GAINSBOROUGH CL
GREEN PARK
MAITLAND AVENUE
MORTLOCK AVE
Works
Mast
MILTON ROAD
COOK CL
SCARSDALE CL
GREEN END
A
47
19
CB4
B
C
Southgates Farm
PKINS CL
ROBERT JENNINGS CL
KENDAL WY
Rec Gnd
SHERBO
NUFFIELD ROAD
PIPPIN DR
St Andrew's CE

13

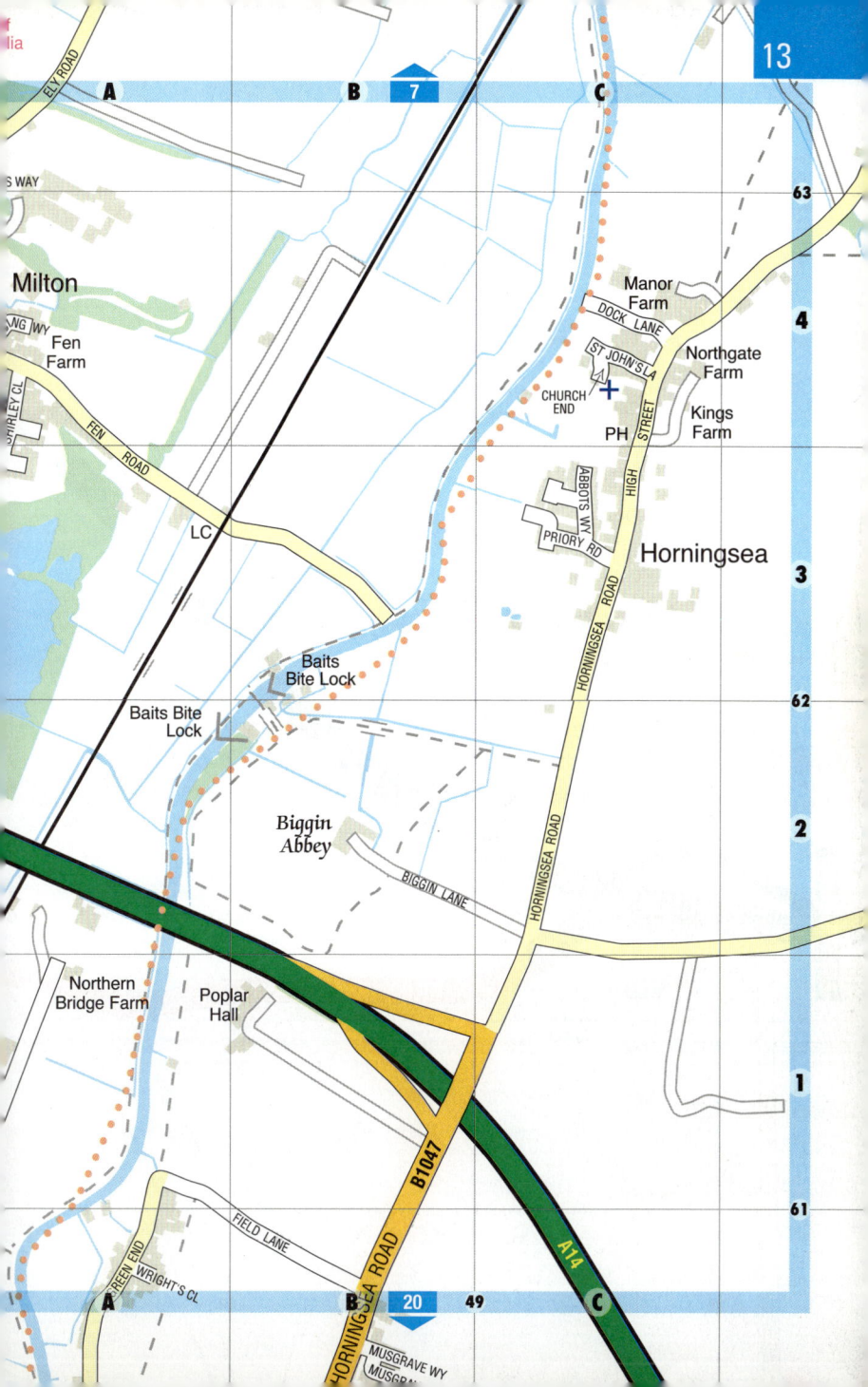

A | B | C

Milton

Fen Farm

FEN ROAD

LC

Baits Bite Lock

Baits Bite Lock

Biggin Abbey

BIGGIN LANE

Northern Bridge Farm

Poplar Hall

FIELD LANE

GREEN END

WRIGHT'S CL

HORNINGSEA ROAD

MUSGRAVE WY

B1047

A14

Manor Farm

DOCK LANE

St John's La

Northgate Farm

CHURCH END

Kings Farm

PH

ABBOTS WY

PRIORY RD

HIGH STREET

HORNINGSEA ROAD

Horningsea

ELY ROAD

SHIRLEY CL

7

20 49

63

4

3

62

2

1

61

14

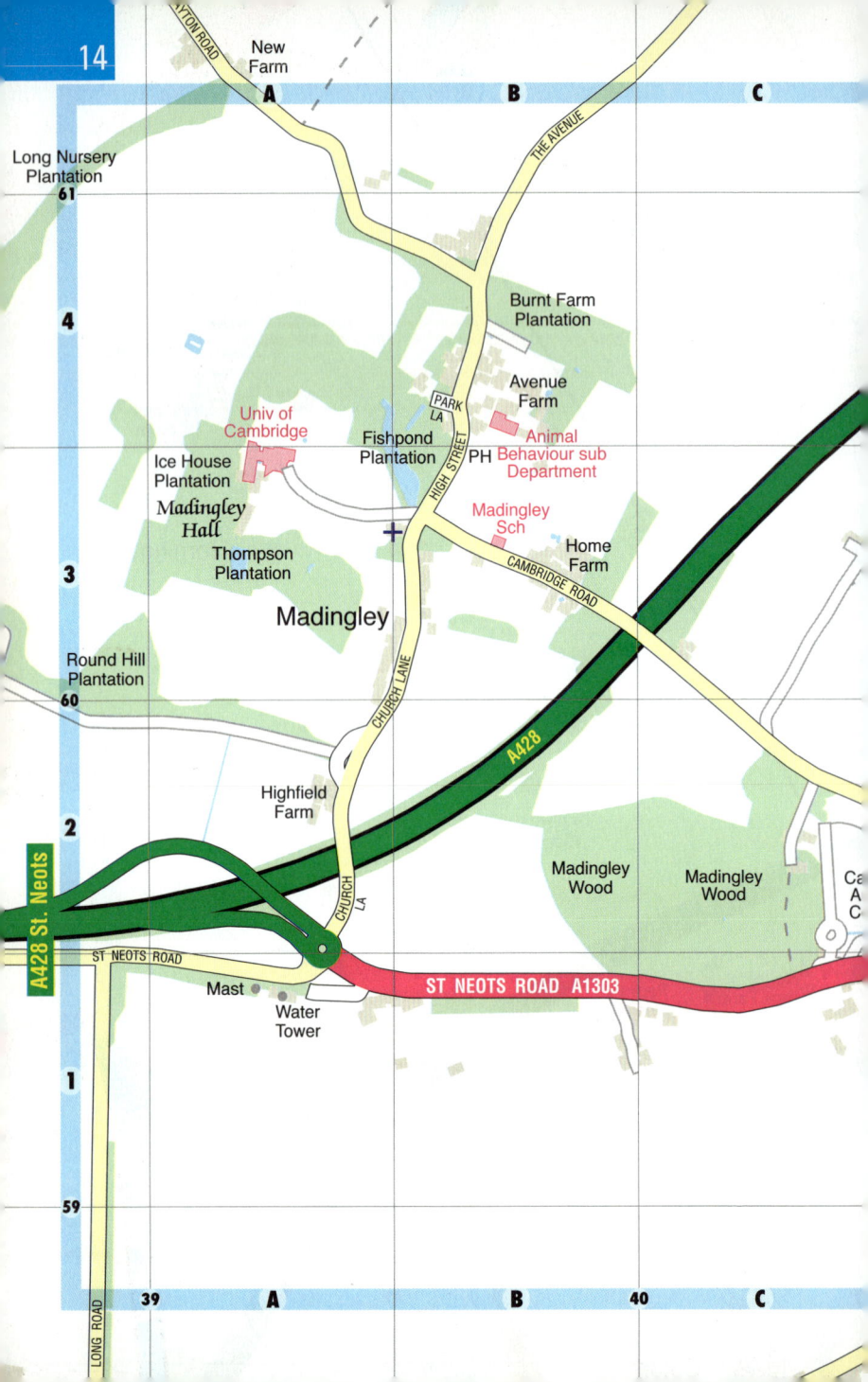

- New Farm
- Long Nursery Plantation
- Burnt Farm Plantation
- THE AVENUE
- Avenue Farm
- Univ of Cambridge
- Ice House Plantation
- PARK LA
- Fishpond Plantation
- HIGH STREET
- PH
- Animal Behaviour sub Department
- Madingley Hall
- Madingley Sch
- Thompson Plantation
- Home Farm
- CAMBRIDGE ROAD
- **Madingley**
- Round Hill Plantation
- CHURCH LANE
- A428
- Highfield Farm
- Madingley Wood
- Madingley Wood
- A428 St. Neots
- CHURCH LA
- ST NEOTS ROAD
- Mast
- Water Tower
- ST NEOTS ROAD A1303
- LONG ROAD

CB3

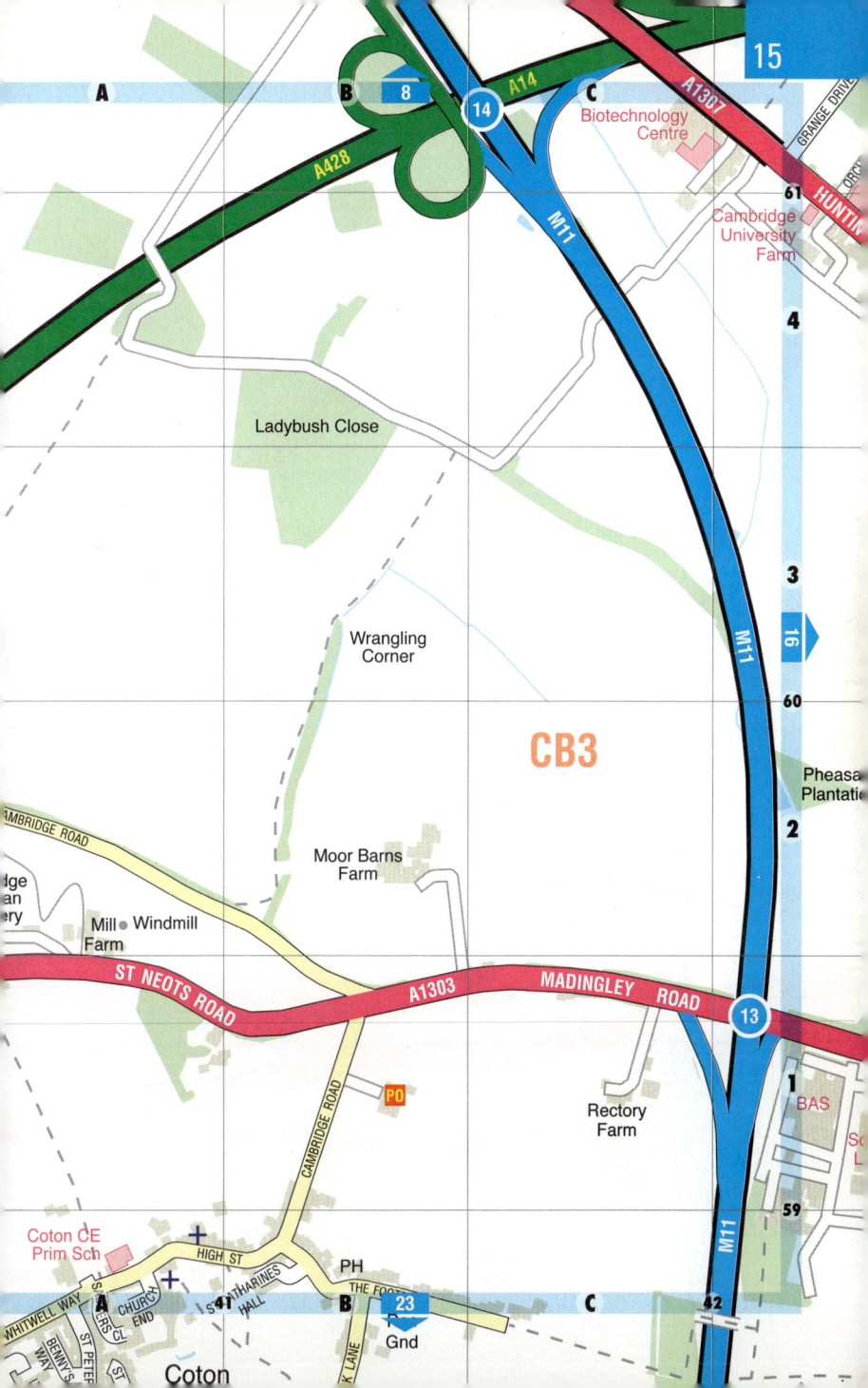

A428
A14
M11
A1307 HUNTINGDON
GRANGE DRIVE

Biotechnology Centre
Cambridge University Farm

Ladybush Close

Wrangling Corner

Pheasant Plantation

Moor Barns Farm

CAMBRIDGE ROAD
Mill Farm • Windmill
ST NEOTS ROAD — A1303 — MADINGLEY ROAD

PO

Rectory Farm

BAS

Coton CE Prim Sch
WHITWELL WAY
BENNY'S WAY
ST PETER'S
CHURCH END
HIGH ST
ST CATHARINES HALL
PH
THE FOOTPATH
K LANE
Rec Gnd

Coton

Map

Grid references: 16, 9, 15, 13, 24, 43, 42, 61, 60, 59, 4, 3, 2, 1

Roads
- A1307 / Huntingdon Road
- A1303 / Dingley Road
- M11
- Grange Ave
- Orchard Drive
- Girton Road
- Wellbrook Wy
- Wilderspin Cl
- Thornton Road
- Thornton Way
- Thornton Close
- St Margaret's Road
- Bandon Rd
- Thornton Ct
- The Brambles
- Whitehouse Lane
- Howes Place
- Lansdowne Road
- Conduit Head Rd
- Bradrushe Fields
- Thompson Ave
- Clerk Maxwell Road
- Hedgerley Cl
- The Lawns
- Perry Ct

Labelled locations
- Biotechnology Centre
- Cambridge University Farm
- Girton Coll
- Playing Fields
- Trinity Farm
- Gravel Hill Farm
- University Department of Ergonomy
- Pheasant Plantation
- Trinity Conduit Head
- P & R
- Bullard Laboratories
- Institute of Astronomy
- Rectory Farm
- BAS
- Schlumberger Laboratories
- Dept of Veterinary Medicine
- Merton Hall Farm
- Computer Laboratory
- Physics Dept
- Emman College Sports Groun
- High Cross

17

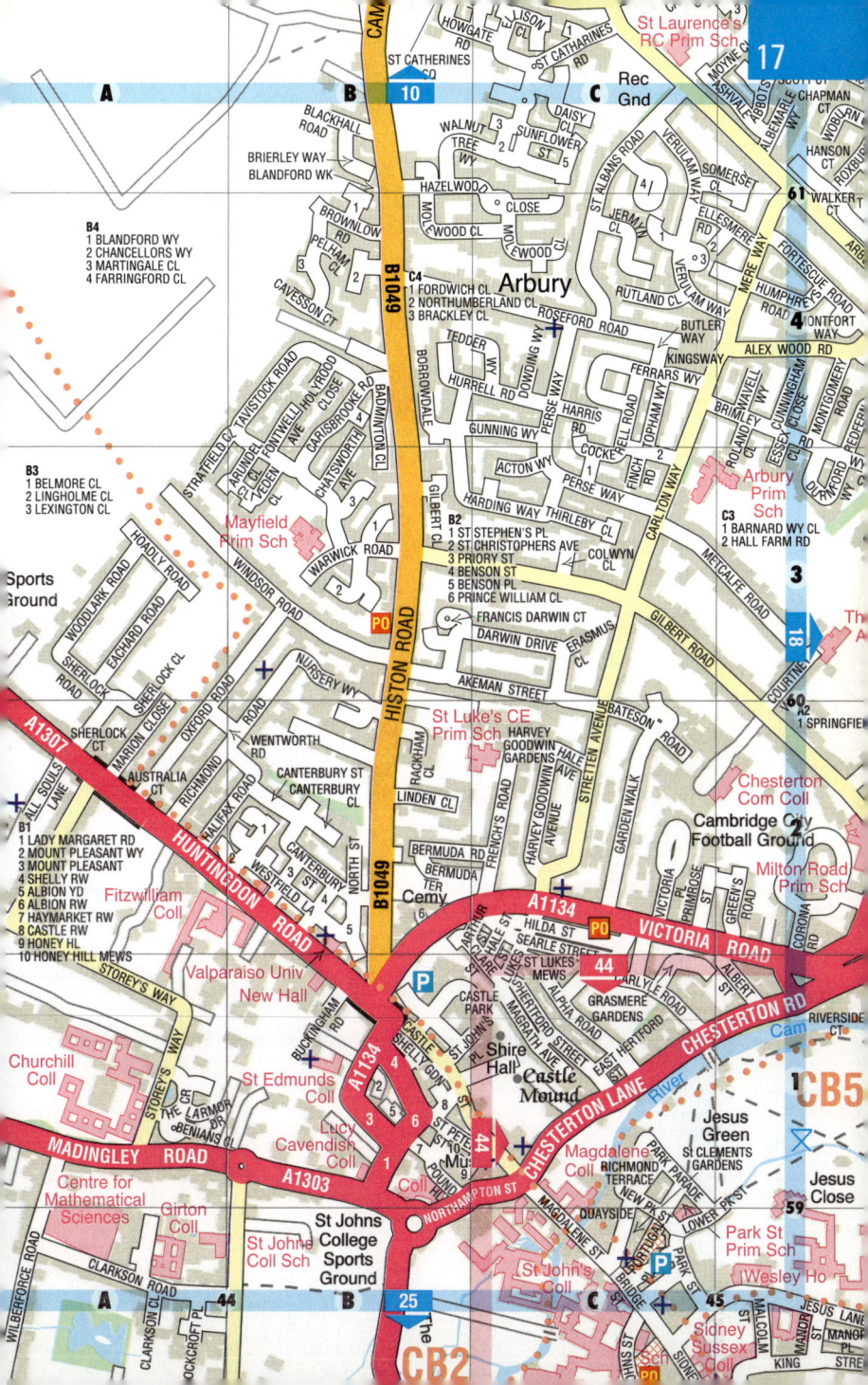

B4
1 BLANDFORD WY
2 CHANCELLORS WY
3 MARTINGALE CL
4 FARRINGFORD CL

B3
1 BELMORE CL
2 LINGHOLME CL
3 LEXINGTON CL

C4
1 FORDWICH CL
2 NORTHUMBERLAND CL
3 BRACKLEY CL

B2
1 ST STEPHEN'S PL
2 ST CHRISTOPHERS AVE
3 PRIORY ST
4 BENSON ST
5 BENSON PL
6 PRINCE WILLIAM CL

C3
1 BARNARD WY CL
2 HALL FARM RD

B1
1 LADY MARGARET RD
2 MOUNT PLEASANT WY
3 MOUNT PLEASANT
4 SHELLY RW
5 ALBION YD
6 ALBION RW
7 HAYMARKET RW
8 CASTLE RW
9 HONEY HL
10 HONEY HILL MEWS

Arbury

St Laurence's RC Prim Sch
Rec Gnd
Arbury Prim Sch
Chesterton Com Coll
Cambridge City Football Ground
Milton Road Prim Sch
St Luke's CE Prim Sch
Fitzwilliam Coll
Valparaiso Univ New Hall
Churchill Coll
St Edmunds Coll
Lucy Cavendish Coll
Centre for Mathematical Sciences
Girton Coll
St Johns Coll Sch
St Johns College Sports Ground
Magdalene Coll
Shire Hall
Castle Mound
St John's Coll
Jesus Green
Jesus Close
Park St Prim Sch
Wesley Ho
Sidney Sussex Coll

CB5
CB2

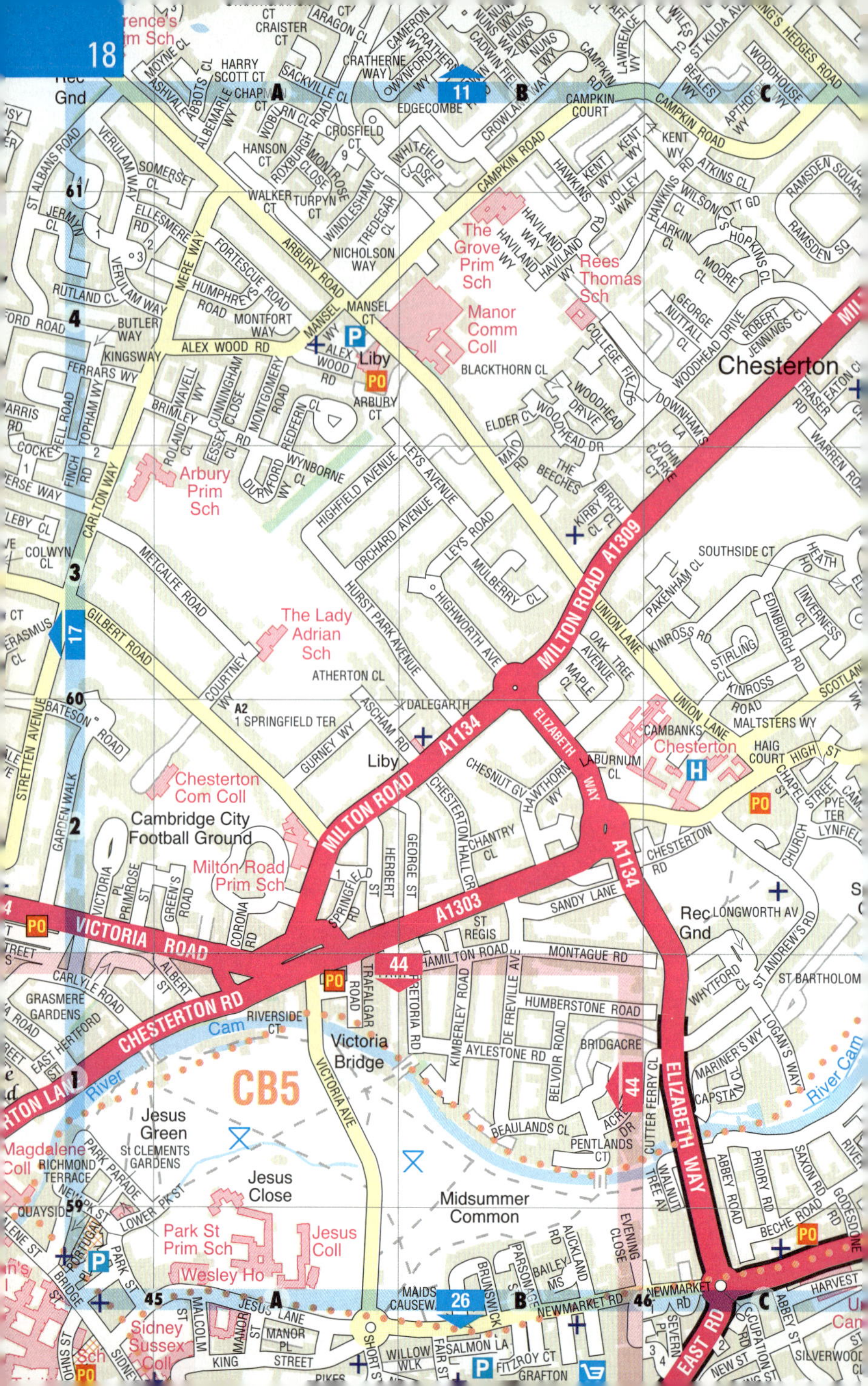

11
A
B
C
Rec Gnd
Chesterton
Harry Scott Ct
Chapman Ct
Moyne Cl
Ashvale
Abbots Cl
Albemarle Wy
Sackville Cl
Aragon Cl
Craister Ct
Cratherne Way
Cameron Wy
Owynford Wy
Nuns Way
Cadwin Field
Edgecombe
Crowland Way
Campkin Rd
Campkin Court
Campkin Road
Lawrence Wy
Wiles Cl
St Kilda Av
Beales Wy
Apthorpe Wy
Woodhouse Wy
King's Hedges Road
Kent Wy
Atkins Cl
Ramsden Square
Ramsden Sq
Wilson Cl
Scott Gd
Hopkins Cl
Larkin Cl
Moore Cl
Jolley Way
Hawkins Rd
Verulam Way
Somerset Cl
St Albans Road
Jermyn Cl
Ellesmere Rd
Rutland Cl
Woburn Cl
Roxburgh Rd
Montrose Close
Hanson Ct
Crosfield Ct
Whitefield Close
Walker Ct
Turpyn Ct
Windlesham Cl
Tredegar Cl
Nicholson Way
Mere Way
Fortescue Road
Humphreys Road
Montfort Way
Arbury Road
Mansel Way
Mansel Ct
The Grove Prim Sch
Haviland Way
Rees Thomas Sch
Manor Comm Coll
College Fields
George Nuttall Cl
Woodhead Drive
Robert Jennings Cl
Butler Way
Kingsway
Alex Wood Rd
Liby
PO
Arbury Ct
Blackthorn Cl
Ferrars Wy
Harris Rd
Cockerell Road
Topham Wy
Wavell Wy
Brimley Cl
Rolands Cl
Cunningham Close
Essex Cl
Montgomery Road
Redfern Cl
Durnford Wy
Wynborne Cl
Finch Rd
Perse Way
Carlton Way
Arbury Prim Sch
Highfield Avenue
Leys Avenue
Leys Road
Orchard Avenue
Elder Cl
Woodhead Dr
Maio Rd
The Beeches
Birch Cl
Kirby Cl
Downham's La
John Clarke Ct
Fraser Rd
Eaton Cl
Warren Road
Apleby Cl
Colwyn Cl
Metcalfe Road
Mulberry Cl
Highworth Ave
Milton Road A1309
Union Lane
Southside Ct
Pakenham Cl
Heath Ho
Edinburgh Rd
Inverness Cl
Kinross Rd
Stirling Cl
Kinross Road
Scotland Rd
Erasmus Cl
17
Gilbert Road
The Lady Adrian Sch
Hurst Park Avenue
Atherton Cl
Courtney Wy
Oak Tree Avenue
Maple Cl
Elizabeth Way
Maltsters Wy
Cambanks
Chesterton
H
Haig Court
High St
Chapel St
Stretten Avenue
Bateson Road
A2
1 Springfield Ter
Ascham Rd
Dalegarth
Gurney Wy
A1134
Chesnut Gv
Hawthorn Wy
Laburnum Cl
Pye Ter
Lynfield
Church St
Garden Walk
Chesterton Com Coll
Cambridge City Football Ground
Milton Road
Chesterton Hall Cr
George St
Herbert St
Springfield Rd
Chantry Cl
Chesterton Rd
Milton Road Prim Sch
Victoria Pl
Primrose St
Green's Road
Corona Rd
A1303
St Regis
Sandy Lane
Rec Gnd
Longworth Av
St Andrew's Rd
Victoria Road
Albert St
Carlyle Road
44
Hamilton Road
Montague Rd
Grasmere Gardens
Chesterton Rd
Trafalgar Road
Pretoria Rd
Kimberley Road
De Freville Ave
Humberstone Road
Whytford Cl
St Bartholomew
Riverside Ct
Cam
East Hertford St
Victoria Bridge
Victoria Ave
Aylestone Rd
Belvoir Road
Bridgacre
Cutter Ferry Cl
Elizabeth Way
Mariner's Wy
Logan's Way
Capstan Cl
River Cam
CB5
River
Jesus Green
St Clements Gardens
Beaulands Cl
Acrefield Dr
Pentlands Ct
Walnut Tree Av
Abbey Road
Priory Rd
Saxon Rd
Godesdone Rd
Beche Road
Magdalene Coll
Richmond Terrace
Park Parade
New Park St
Lower Park St
Jesus Close
Midsummer Common
Quayside
59
Portugal Pl
Park St
Park St Prim Sch
Jesus Coll
Wesley Ho
Auckland Rd
Bailey Ms
Parsonage St
Brunswick
Evening Close
Newmarket Rd
45
Jesus Lane
Maids Causeway
26
Newmarket Rd
46
Harvest
East Rd
Abbey St
Occupation Rd
Sidney Sussex Coll
Malcolm St
Manor St
Manor Pl
King Street
Short St
Willow Wlk
Salmon La
Fair St
Fitzroy Ct
Grafton
Severn Pl
New St
Silverwood Cl
Sch
PO
1
2
3
4
60
61

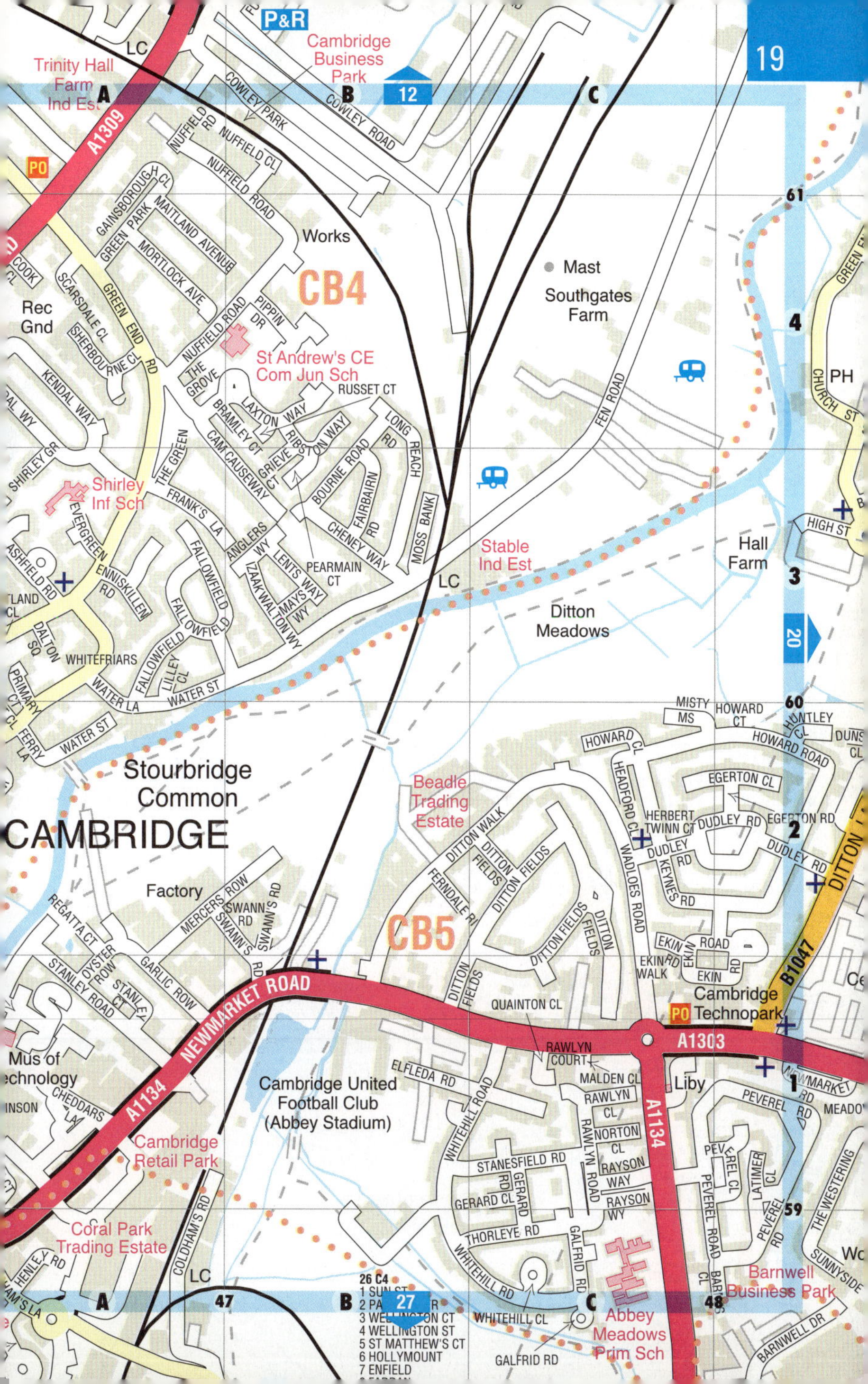
P&R
Cambridge Business Park
Trinity Hall Farm Ind Est
A1309
PO
COWLEY PARK
COWLEY ROAD
NUFFIELD RD
NUFFIELD CL
NUFFIELD ROAD
GAINSBOROUGH CL
GREEN PARK
MAITLAND AVENUE
MORTLOCK AVE
Works
CB4
Mast
Southgates Farm
COOK CL
SCARSDALE CL
GREEN END RD
SHERBOURNE CL
Rec Gnd
NUFFIELD ROAD
PIPPIN DR
St Andrew's CE Com Jun Sch
THE GROVE
RUSSET CT
LAXTON WAY
BRAMLEY CT
RIBSTON WAY
LONG REACH RD
FEN ROAD
KENDAL WAY
SHIRLEY GR
THE GREEN
CAM CAUSEWAY
GRIEVE CT
BOURNE ROAD
FAIRBAIRN RD
MOSS BANK
Shirley Inf Sch
FRANK'S LA
EVERGREEN
ANGLERS WY
CHENEY WAY
Stable Ind Est
Hall Farm
HIGH ST
CHURCH ST
PH
ASHFIELD RD
ENNISKILLEN RD
FALLOWFIELD
IZAAK WALTON WY
LENTS WAY
MAYS WY
PEARMAIN CT
LC
Ditton Meadows
DALTON SQ
WHITEFRIARS
LILLEY CL
WATER LA
WATER ST
PRIMARY CT
FERRY LA
Stourbridge Common
CAMBRIDGE
Beadle Trading Estate
MISTY MS
HOWARD CT
HUNTLEY CL
HOWARD CL
HOWARD ROAD
DUNS CL
EGERTON CL
EGERTON RD
HEADFORD CL
HERBERT TWINN CT
DUDLEY RD
DUDLEY RD
DITTON WALK
DITTON FIELDS
FERNDALE RI
DITTON FIELDS
WADLOES ROAD
KEYNES RD
Factory
MERCERS ROW
SWANN'S RD
REGATTA CT
OYSTER ROW
STANLEY ROAD
STANLEY CT
GARLIC ROW
CB5
EKIN ROAD
EKIN WALK
EKIN RD
B1047
DITTON
NEWMARKET ROAD
QUAINTON CL
Cambridge Technopark
A1303
RAWLYN COURT
MALDEN CL
Liby
NEWMARKET RD
PEVEREL RD
MEADO
Mus of Technology
CHEDDARS LA
A1134
Cambridge United Football Club (Abbey Stadium)
ELFLEDA RD
WHITEHILL ROAD
RAWLYN CL
NORTON CL
RAWLYN ROAD
A1134
Cambridge Retail Park
STANESFIELD RD
GERARD RD
RAYSON WAY
RAYSON WY
PEVEREL CL
LATIMER CL
PEVEREL ROAD
PEVEREL RD
THE WESTERING
SUNNYSIDE
GERARD CL
THORLEYE RD
Coral Park Trading Estate
COLDHAM'S RD
GALFRID RD
WHITEHILL RD
HENLEY RD
Barnwell Business Park
WHITEHILL CL
Abbey Meadows Prim Sch
BARNWELL DR
GALFRID RD
26 C4
1 SUN ST
2 PARK ... R
3 WELLINGTON CT
4 WELLINGTON ST
5 ST MATTHEW'S CT
6 HOLLYMOUNT
7 ENFIELD
A
B
C
12
20
27
61
4
3
60
2
1
59
47
48

20

Fen Ditton

- Mast
- uthgates Farm
- Fen Road
- Green End
- Wright's Cl
- Field Lane
- Horningsea Road B1047
- Musgrave Wy
- Musgrave Wy
- A14
- Church St
- Stanbury
- PH
- Cemy
- Bakery Cl
- High St
- Hall Farm
- Musgrave Farm
- High Street
- PO
- PH
- Fen Ditton CP Sch
- Home Farm
- Shepherd's Cl
- High St
- itton adows
- Misty Ms
- Howard Ct
- Huntley
- Dunsm Cl
- Howard Road
- Fison Rd
- Tip Tree Cl
- Howard
- Headford
- Egerton Cl
- Ann's Rd
- Dennis Rd
- Herbert
- Twinn Ct
- Dudley Rd
- Egerton Rd
- Velos Walk
- Thorpe Way
- Dudley
- Keynes Rd
- Ditton Lane B1047
- The Rodings
- Hadleigh Ct
- Brentwood Court
- Fields
- Ditton
- Fields
- Ekin Road
- Ekin Walk
- Ekin
- Loughton Ct
- Ongar Ct
- Cemetery
- Jack Warren Gn
- Cambridge Technopark
- PO
- Works
- Greenhouse Farm
- P&R
- WLYN OURT
- Malden
- Rawlyn Cl
- Libby
- Newmarket Rd
- A1303
- A1134
- Norton Cl
- Peverel Rd
- Meadowlands Rd
- Newmarket Road A1303
- Rawlyn Road
- Rayson Way
- Pev Latimer Cl
- The Homing
- Rayson Wy
- Peverel Rd
- Peverel Rd
- Thetford Tr
- The Westering
- Galfrid Rd
- Sunnyside
- Cambridge Airport
- Works
- Abbey Meadows Prim Sch
- Barnwell Business Park
- Barnwell Dr

A2
1. Rachel Cl
2. Leonard Cl
3. Helen Cl
4. Bergholt Cl
5. Coggeshall Cl
6. Brentwood Cl
7. Chigwell Ct

21

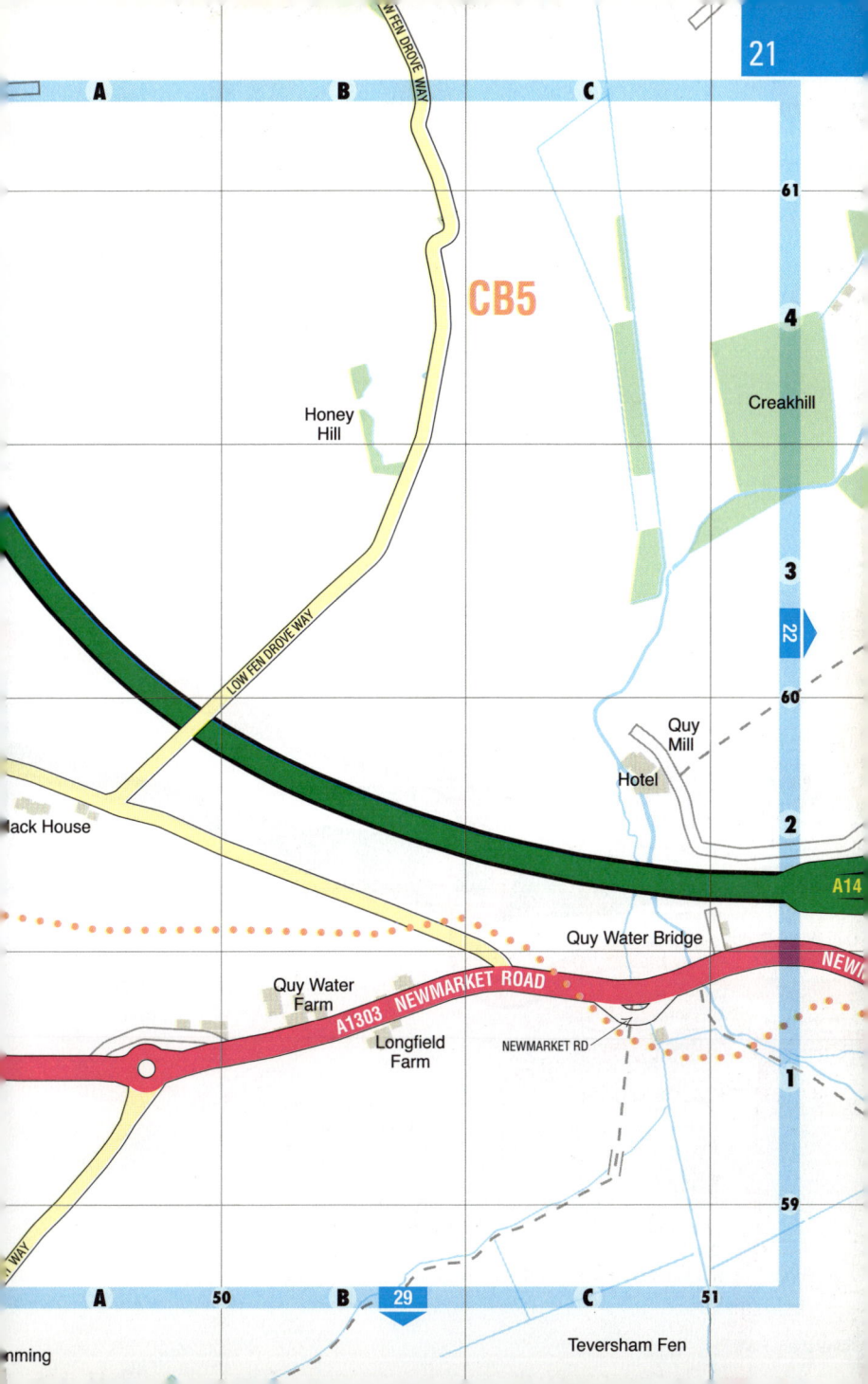

CB5

W FEN DROVE WAY

Honey Hill

Creakhill

LOW FEN DROVE WAY

22

Quy Mill
Hotel

A14

ack House

Quy Water Bridge

Quy Water Farm

A1303 NEWMARKET ROAD

NEWM

Longfield Farm

NEWMARKET RD

nming

Teversham Fen

22

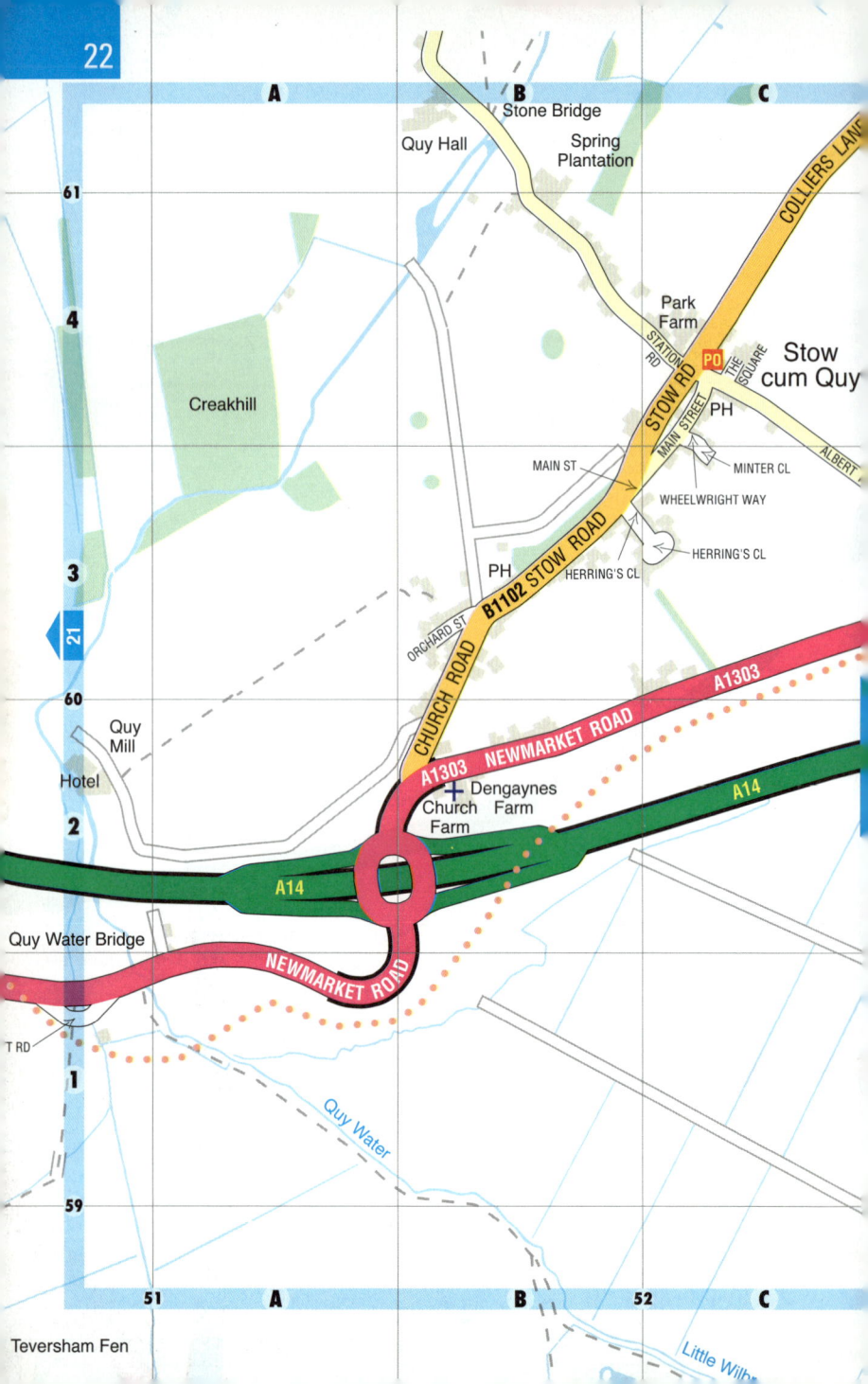

Stow cum Quy

- Stone Bridge
- Quy Hall
- Spring Plantation
- Creakhill
- Park Farm
- STATION RD
- COLLIERS LANE
- STOW RD
- THE SQUARE
- PO
- MAIN STREET
- PH
- MAIN ST
- MINTER CL
- WHEELWRIGHT WAY
- ALBERT
- PH
- B1102 STOW ROAD
- HERRING'S CL
- HERRING'S CL
- ORCHARD ST
- CHURCH ROAD
- A1303 NEWMARKET ROAD
- A1303
- A14
- Quy Mill
- Hotel
- Dengaynes Farm
- Church Farm
- A14
- Quy Water Bridge
- NEWMARKET ROAD
- T RD
- Quy Water
- Teversham Fen
- Little Wilb...

A
B
15
C
Rectory Farm
BAS
59
Coton CE Prim Sch
HIGH ST
CAMBRIDGE ROAD
PH
THE FOOTPATH
ST CATHARINES HALL
CHURCH END
SADLERS CL
WHITWELL WAY
Rec Gnd
M11
4
Harcam
Coton
BENNY'S WAY
ST PETER'S ROAD
ST JOHN'S ROAD
DALE CL
SILVERDALE AVE
SILVERDALE AVE
BROOKFIELD RD
Manor Farm
BROOK LANE
GRANTCHESTER ROAD
Bin Brook
3
24
58
2
M11
ANGER AREA
1
Dumpling Farm
GRANTCHESTER ROAD
57
Rifle Range
A
41
B
30
Haggis Farm
C
M11
42
TON RD

24

Rectory Farm

A BAS
Schlumberger Laboratories

16 B Dept of Veterinary Medicine

Merton Hall Farm

Computer Laboratory **C**

HEDGERLEY CL

Emma Colleg Sport Grou

59

High Cross

J J THOMPSON AVE

CLERK MAXWELL ROAD

LYTE LAWNS

PERRY CT

Physics Dept

4

Harcamlow Way

M11

3

23

CB3

Corpus Sports

GOUGH WY

DANE DR

58

WOOTTON WY

Corpu Colleg Gr

GOUGH WY

PENARTH PL

GOUGH WAY

STUKEL CL

2

Laundry Farm

A603

BARTON RD

Sports Ground

Kings Coll

CROF

1

Dumpling Farm

M11

57

arm **42 A** **31 B** 43 **C**

BARTON RD

CB3

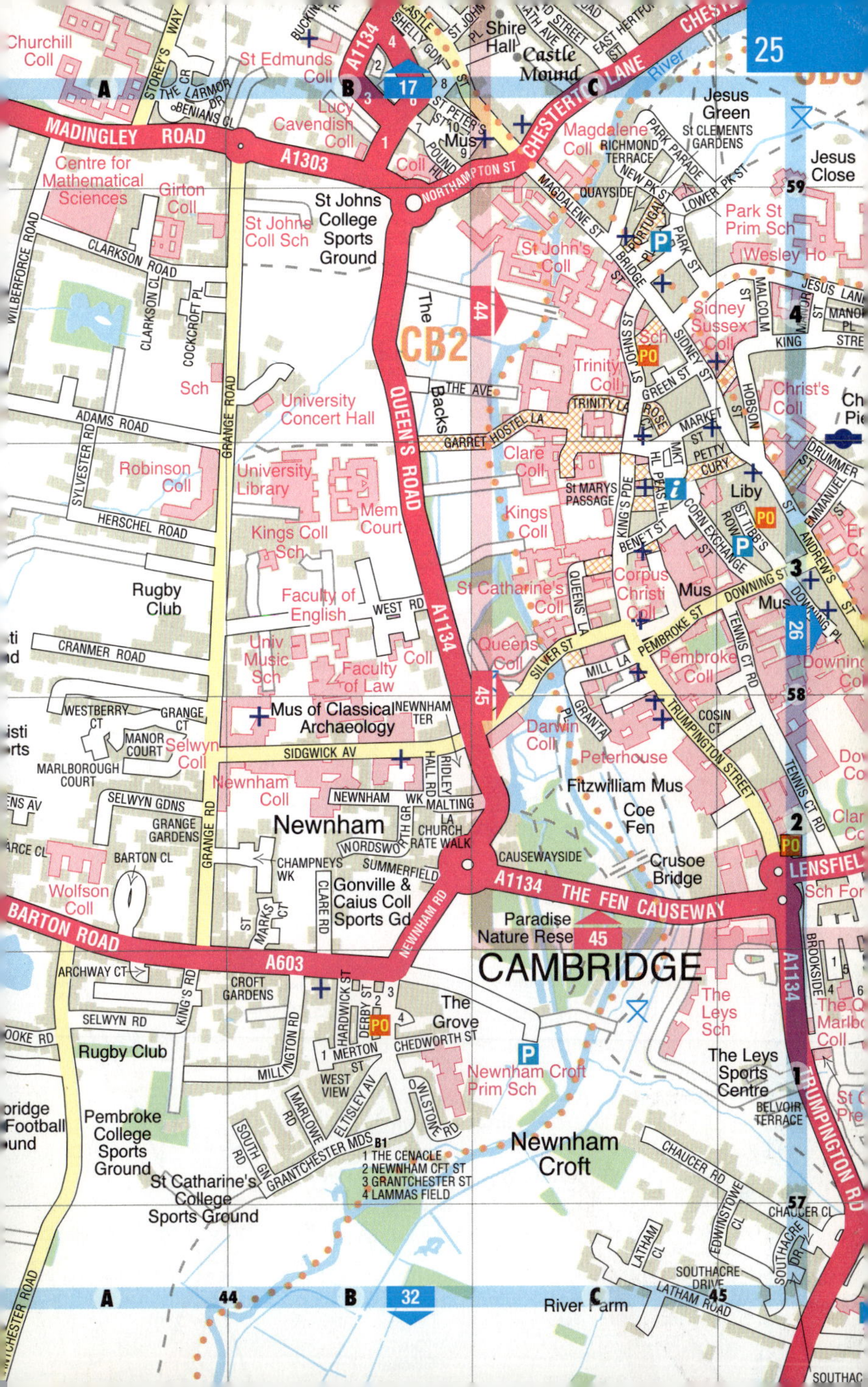
Churchill Coll
St Edmunds Coll
Lucy Cavendish Coll
Shire Hall
Castle Mound
Jesus Green
Jesus Close
MADINGLEY ROAD
A1303
A1134
CHESTERTON LANE
River Cam
Magdalene Coll
ST CLEMENTS GARDENS
RICHMOND TERRACE
PARK PARADE
NEW PK ST
LOWER PK ST
QUAYSIDE
NORTHAMPTON ST
MAGDALENE ST
BRIDGE ST
PORTUGAL PL
PARK ST
Park St Prim Sch
Wesley Ho
Centre for Mathematical Sciences
Girton Coll
St Johns Coll Sch
St Johns College Sports Ground
St John's Coll
CLARKSON ROAD
CLARKSON CL
COCKCROFT PL
WILBERFORCE ROAD
The Backs
CB2
44
Sidney Sussex Coll
MALCOLM ST
JESUS LANE
MANOR PL
KING ST
Trinity Coll
ST JOHNS ST
SIDNEY ST
HOBSON ST
Christ's Coll
GREEN ST
TRINITY LA
ROSE CRES
MARKET ST
PETTY CURY
DRUMMER ST
Sch
University Concert Hall
THE AVE
GARRET HOSTEL LA
QUEEN'S ROAD
ADAMS ROAD
GRANGE ROAD
SYLVESTER RD
Robinson Coll
University Library
Mem Court
Clare Coll
ST MARYS PASSAGE
KING'S PDE
MKT HL
PEAS HL
Liby
CORN EXCHANGE ST
ST TIBB'S ROW
EMMANUEL ST
ST ANDREW'S ST
HERSCHEL ROAD
Kings Coll Sch
Kings Coll
BENE'T ST
Rugby Club
Faculty of English
WEST RD
St Catharine's Coll
QUEENS' LA
Corpus Christi Coll
Mus
DOWNING ST
DOWNING PL
26
CRANMER ROAD
Univ Music Sch
Faculty of Law
Coll
Queens' Coll
SILVER ST
MILL LA
PEMBROKE ST
TENNIS CT RD
Pembroke Coll
Downing Coll
WESTBERRY CT
GRANGE CT
MANOR COURT
Mus of Classical Archaeology
NEWNHAM TER
45
Darwin Coll
GRANTA PL
TRUMPINGTON STREET
COSIN CT
58
MARLBOROUGH COURT
Selwyn Coll
SIDGWICK AV
HALL RD
RIDLEY
Peterhouse
Fitzwilliam Mus
SELWYN GDNS
Newnham Coll
NEWNHAM WK
MALTING LA
CHURCH RATE WALK
Coe Fen
GRANGE GARDENS
Newnham
WORDSWORTH GR
CAUSEWAYSIDE
Crusoe Bridge
BARTON CL
CHAMPNEYS WK
SUMMERFIELD
LENSFIELD
Wolfson Coll
Gonville & Caius Coll Sports Gd
CLARE RD
ST MARKS CT
NEWNHAM RD
A1134 THE FEN CAUSEWAY
Paradise Nature Rese
Sch For
BARTON ROAD
A603
CAMBRIDGE
BROOKSIDE
ARCHWAY CT
CROFT GARDENS
KING'S RD
HARDWICK ST
DERBY ST
The Grove
PO
The Leys Sch
The Q Marlbo Coll
SELWYN RD
MILLINGTON RD
MERTON ST
CHEDWORTH ST
P
Rugby Club
WEST VIEW
Newnham Croft Prim Sch
The Leys Sports Centre
BELVOIR TERRACE
ELTISLEY AV
MARLOWE RD
OWLSTONE RD
St Pre
Pembroke College Sports Ground
SOUTH GN RD
GRANTCHESTER MDS
B1
1 THE CENACLE
2 NEWNHAM CFT ST
3 GRANTCHESTER ST
4 LAMMAS FIELD
Newnham Croft
CHAUCER RD
TRUMPINGTON RD
St Catharine's College Sports Ground
EDWINSTOWE CL
57
CHAUCER CL
LATHAM CL
SOUTHACRE DR
SOUTHACRE DRIVE
LATHAM ROAD
River Farm
GRANTCHESTER ROAD
A
B
C
32
1
2
3
4
59

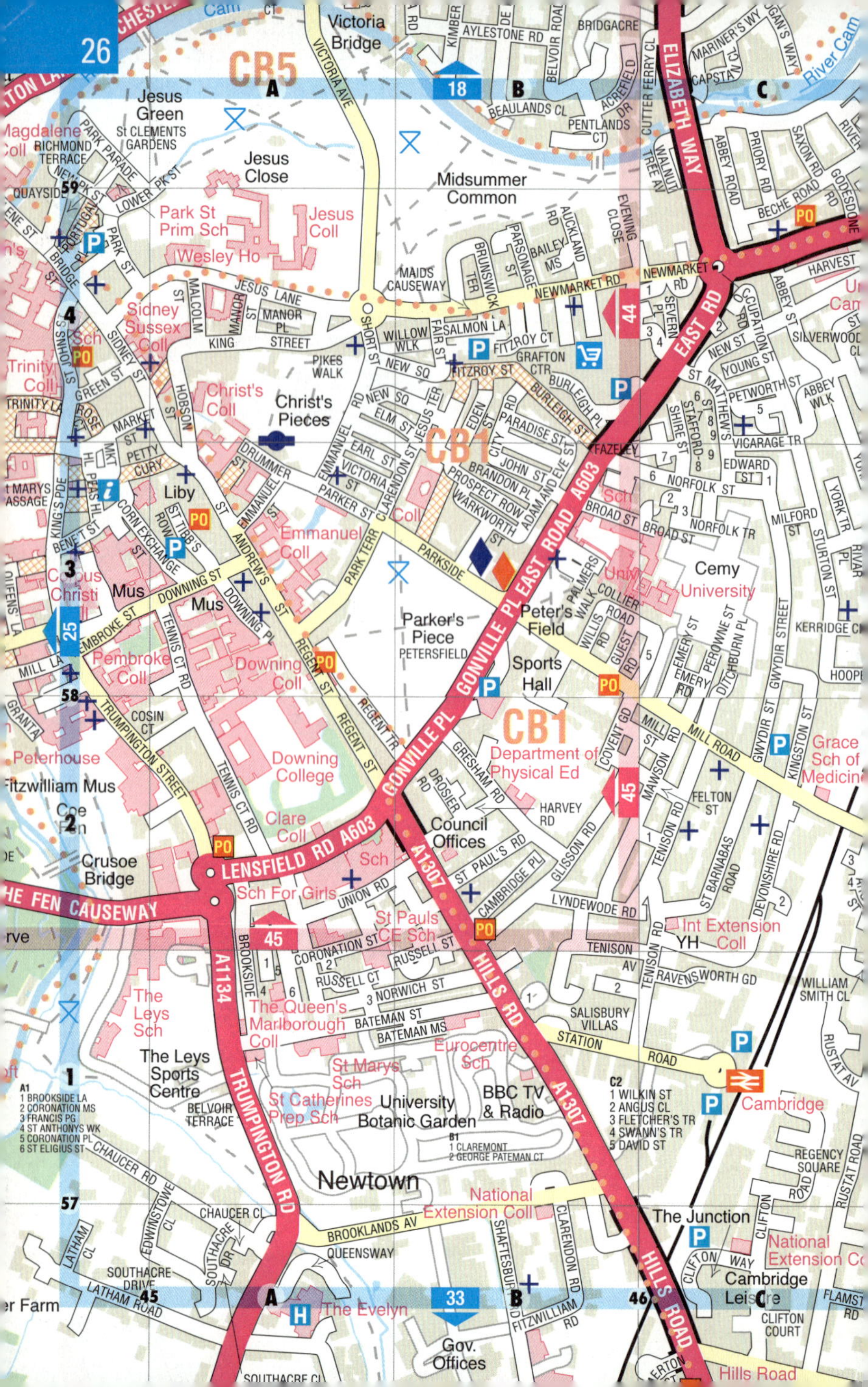
CB5
A
B
C
18
Victoria Bridge
Victoria Ave
Aylestone Rd
Belvoir Road
Kimber
Bridgacre
Beaulands Cl
Pentlands Ct
Acrefield Dr
Cutter Ferry Cl
Elizabeth Way
Mariner's Wy
Capstan Cl
River Cam
Jesus Green
St Clements Gardens
Magdalene Coll
Richmond Terrace
Park Parade
New Park St
Quayside
Lower Pk St
Jesus Close
Midsummer Common
Walnut Tree Av
Abbey Road
Priory Rd
Saxon Rd
Godesdone Rd
Beche Road
Park St Prim Sch
Jesus Coll
Wesley Ho
Portugal Pl
Park St
Bridge St
Maids Causeway
Brunswick Ter
Parsonage St
Bailey Ms
Auckland Rd
Evening Close
Newmarket Rd
Harvest
Jesus Lane
Manor St
Manor Pl
Malcolm St
Sidney Sussex Coll
King Street
Short St
Willow Wlk
Fair St
Salmon La
Fitzroy Ct
Grafton Ctr
Burleigh St
Fitzroy St
Burleigh Pl
New Sq
Pikes Walk
Trinity Coll
St John's St
Sidney St
Green St
Hobson St
Christ's Coll
Christ's Pieces
Trinity La
Rose Cres
Market St
Petty Cury
Mkt Hl
Peas Hl
Drummer St
Emmanuel Rd
Earl St
Elm St
Jesus Ter
Eden St
City Rd
Paradise St
John St
Brandon Pl
Prospect Row
Adam and Eve St
Warkworth St
Victoria St
Parker St
Clarendon St
CB1
Fazeley
East Rd
Occupation Rd
Abbey St
Silverwood Cl
New St
Young St
St Matthew's St
Petworth St
Abbey Wlk
Shire St
Stafford St
Vicarage Tr
Edward St
Norfolk St
Broad St
Norfolk Tr
Milford St
York Tr
Sturton St
Gwydir Street
Kerridge Cl
Hooper
St Marys Passage
King's Pde
Liby
St Tibb's Row
Corn Exchange St
Bene't St
Emmanuel St
St Andrew's St
Emmanuel Coll
Park Terr
Parkside
Coll
Sch
Gonville Pl
East Road A603
Palmers Walk
Collier Road
Univ
Cemy
University
Corpus Christi Coll
Mus
Downing St
Downing Pl
Pembroke St
Pembroke Coll
Tennis Ct Rd
Regent St
Parker's Piece
Petersfield
Peter's Field
Willis Rd
Guest Rd
Emery St
Emery Rd
Perowne St
Ditchburn Pl
Mill La
Downing Coll
Sports Hall
Mill Rd
Mill Road
Gwydir St
Kingston St
Grace Sch of Medicine
Granta Pl
Cosin Ct
Trumpington Street
Regent Tr
Covent Gd
Mawson Rd
Felton St
Peterhouse
Fitzwilliam Mus
Coe Fen
Downing College
Department of Physical Ed
Gresham Rd
Drosier Rd
Harvey Rd
Tenison Rd
St Barnabas Road
Devonshire Rd
Crusoe Bridge
Clare Coll
Lensfield Rd A603
Council Offices
St Paul's Rd
Cambridge Pl
Glisson Rd
The Fen Causeway
Sch For Girls
Union Rd
Lyndewode Rd
Int Extension Coll
YH
Brookside
Coronation St
St Pauls CE Sch
Russell St
A1307
Hills Rd
Tenison Av
Ravensworth Gd
William Smith Cl
A1134
Russell Ct
Norwich St
The Queen's Marlborough Coll
Bateman St
Bateman Ms
Salisbury Villas
Station Road
Rustat Av
The Leys Sch
Eurocentre Sch
The Leys Sports Centre
St Marys Sch
St Catherines Prep Sch
University Botanic Garden
BBC TV & Radio
Cambridge
Belvoir Terrace
Trumpington Rd
A1
1 Brookside La
2 Coronation Ms
3 Francis Pg
4 St Anthonys Wk
5 Coronation Pl
6 St Eligius St
C2
1 Wilkin St
2 Angus Cl
3 Fletcher's Tr
4 Swann's Tr
5 David St
B1
1 Claremont
2 George Pateman Ct
Regency Square
Rustat Road
Chaucer Rd
Newtown
National Extension Coll
Edwinstowe Cl
Chaucer Cl
Southacre Dr
Clarendon Rd
Shaftesbury Rd
Clifton Road
The Junction
Latham Cl
Brooklands Av
Queensway
Southacre Drive
Latham Road
Clifton Way
Cambridge Leisure
National Extension Coll
Flamsteed Rd
The Evelyn
33
Fitzwilliam Rd
Clifton Court
Gov. Offices
Hills Road
Southacre Cl
44
45
25
59
58
57
45
46
4
3
2
1
PO

27

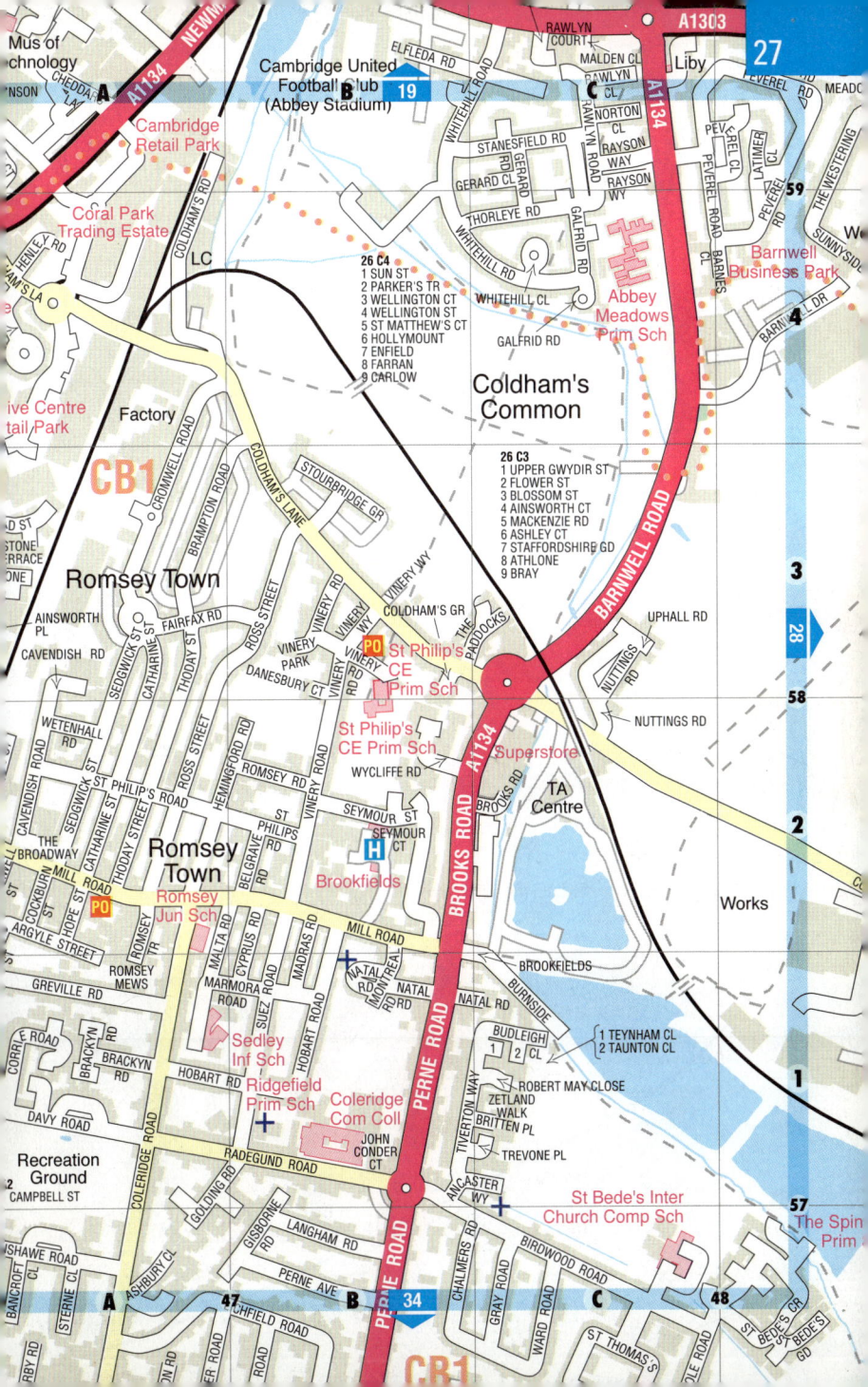

A1303

Mus of chnology — CHEDDA LA — NEWM — A1134 — RAWLYN COURT — MALDEN CL — Liby — EVEREL RD — MEAD

A — NSON — B Cambridge United Football Club (Abbey Stadium) — 19 — ELFLEDA RD — C RAWLYN CL — A1134 — NORTON CL — PEV — REL CL — LATIMER RD — PEVEREL RD — THE WESTERING

Cambridge Retail Park — WHITEHILL ROAD — STANESFIELD RD — GERARD RD — RAYSON WAY — RAYSON WY — BARNES — 59

Coral Park Trading Estate — GERARD CL — THORLEYE RD — GALFRID RD — WHITEHILL RD — Abbey Meadows Prim Sch — Barnwell Business Park — SUNNYSIDE

ive Centre tail Park — LC — **26 C4**
1 SUN ST
2 PARKER'S TR
3 WELLINGTON CT
4 WELLINGTON ST
5 ST MATTHEW'S CT
6 HOLLYMOUNT
7 ENFIELD
8 FARRAN
9 CARLOW

WHITEHILL CL — GALFRID RD — BARNT — L DR — 4

HENLEY RD — HAM'S LA — Factory — COLDHAM'S RD — CROMWELL ROAD — BRAMPTON ROAD — COLDHAM'S LANE — STOURBRIDGE GR — Coldham's Common

CB1

26 C3
1 UPPER GWYDIR ST
2 FLOWER ST
3 BLOSSOM ST
4 AINSWORTH CT
5 MACKENZIE RD
6 ASHLEY CT
7 STAFFORDSHIRE GD
8 ATHLONE
9 BRAY

Romsey Town — AINSWORTH PL — CAVENDISH RD — WETENHALL RD — SEDGWICK ST — CATHARINE ST — FAIRFAX RD — THODAY ST — ROSS STREET — VINERY RD — VINERY PARK — DANESBURY CT — VINERY WY — COLDHAM'S GR — THE PADDOCKS — BARNWELL ROAD — UPHALL RD — 3

PO — St Philip's CE Prim Sch — NUTTINGS RD — 28 — 58

St Philip's CE Prim Sch — NUTTINGS RD

THE BROADWAY — SEDGWICK ST — CATHARINE ST — THODAY ST — ST PHILIP'S ROAD — ROSS STREET — HEMINGFORD RD — ROMSEY TERR — PHILIP ST — VINERY RD — SEYMOUR ST — WYCLIFFE RD — BROOKS RD — A1134 — Superstore — TA Centre — Works — 2

Romsey Town — BELGRAVE RD — SEYMOUR CT — H Brookfields

MILL ROAD — PO Romsey Jun Sch — ARGYLE STREET — HOPE ST — COCKBURN ST — MILL ROAD — ROMSEY MEWS — GREVILLE RD — MALTA RD — CYPRUS RD — MADRAS RD — SUEZ RD — MARMORA ROAD — HOBART RD — NATAL REA — MILL RD — NATAL RD — Sedley Inf Sch — BROOKS RD — NATAL RD — BURNSIDE — BROOKFIELDS — 1 TEYNHAM CL — 2 TAUNTON CL

CORRIE RD — BRACKYN RD — BRACKYN RD — DAVY ROAD — COLERIDGE RD — HOBART RD — Ridgefield Prim Sch — Coleridge Com Coll — PERNE ROAD — BUDLEIGH 1 2 CL — ROBERT MAY CLOSE — ZETLAND WALK — BRITTEN PL — TREVONE PL

Recreation Ground — CAMPBELL ST — COLERIDGE RD — GOLDING RD — RADEGUND ROAD — JOHN CONDER CT — ANCASTER WY — TIVERTON WAY — St Bede's Inter Church Comp Sch — The Spin Prim Sch — 57

SHAWE ROAD — BANCROFT CL — STERNE RD — ABY RD — ASHBURY CL — GISBORNE RD — LANGHAM RD — PERNE AVE — CHFIELD ROAD — A 47 — B 34 — PERNE ROAD — CHALMERS RD — GRAY ROAD — BIRDWOOD ROAD — WARD ROAD — C 48 — OLE ROAD — ST BEDE'S CR — BEDE'S GD — ST THOMAS'S

CB1

A1303
Works
P&R
NEWMARKET RD
PEVEREL RD
MEADOWLANDS RD
20
NEWMARKET ROAD
A1303
A
B
C
RAWLYN CL
NORTON CL
RAWLYN ROAD
RAYSON WAY
RAYSON WY
59
A1134
PEVEREL CL
LATIMER CL
PEVEREL ROAD
PEVEREL RD
THE HOMING
THE WESTERING
THETFORD TR
Cambridge Airport
Works
SUNNYSIDE
BARNES CL
GALFRID RD
Barnwell Business Park
Abbey Meadows Prim Sch
4
BARNWELL DR
DIR ST
CT RD
IRE GD
BARNWELL ROAD
3
UPHALL RD
27
NUTTINGS RD
58
NUTTINGS RD
2
Works
COLDHAM'S LANE
PH
HATHERDENE CL
ROSEMARY LA
REILLY WY
MARCH LANE
CHURCH END
MARCH LA
TEVERSHAM DRIFT
BRITANNIC WY
KATHLEEN ELLIOT WAY
WOLSEY WY
IVER CL
NEWELL WALK
QUEEN'S MD
NEALE CL
NEALE CL
CHURCH END
TEVERSHAM DRIFT
TEVERSHAM DRIFT
CHERRY HINTON RD
DOLPHIN CL
CARIBOU WY
BUFFALO WY
MANDRILL CL
CAPUCHIN CT
THE LYNX
1 TEYNHAM CL
2 TAUNTON CL
1
Y CLOSE
ORCHARD EST
HIGH ST
KELSEY CR
LEYBURN CL
SABLE CL
ROEDEER CL
HAYSTER DR
RAILWAY ST
FERNLEA CL
TENBY CL
BURNHAM CL
St Bede's Inter Ch Comp Sch
57
The Spinney Prim Sch
HARCOMBE RD
HAYSTER DR
Cherry Hinton CE Prim Sch
BLISS WY
FULBOURN OLD DRIFT
Cherry Hinton Com Jun Sch
LC
HIGHDENE RD
WELSTEAD RD
TAMARIN GD
ROAD
48
A
RICKARD CL
DOGGETT RD
35
B
49
SUNMEAD WALK
LISLE WALK
RUSH GR
C
ST BEDE'S CR
ST BEDE'S GD
ST THOMAS'S
SIDNEY FARM RD
CHELWOOD RD
CHARTFIELD RD
HIGH STREET
FISHER'S
WENVOE CL
SPEEDWELL CL

29

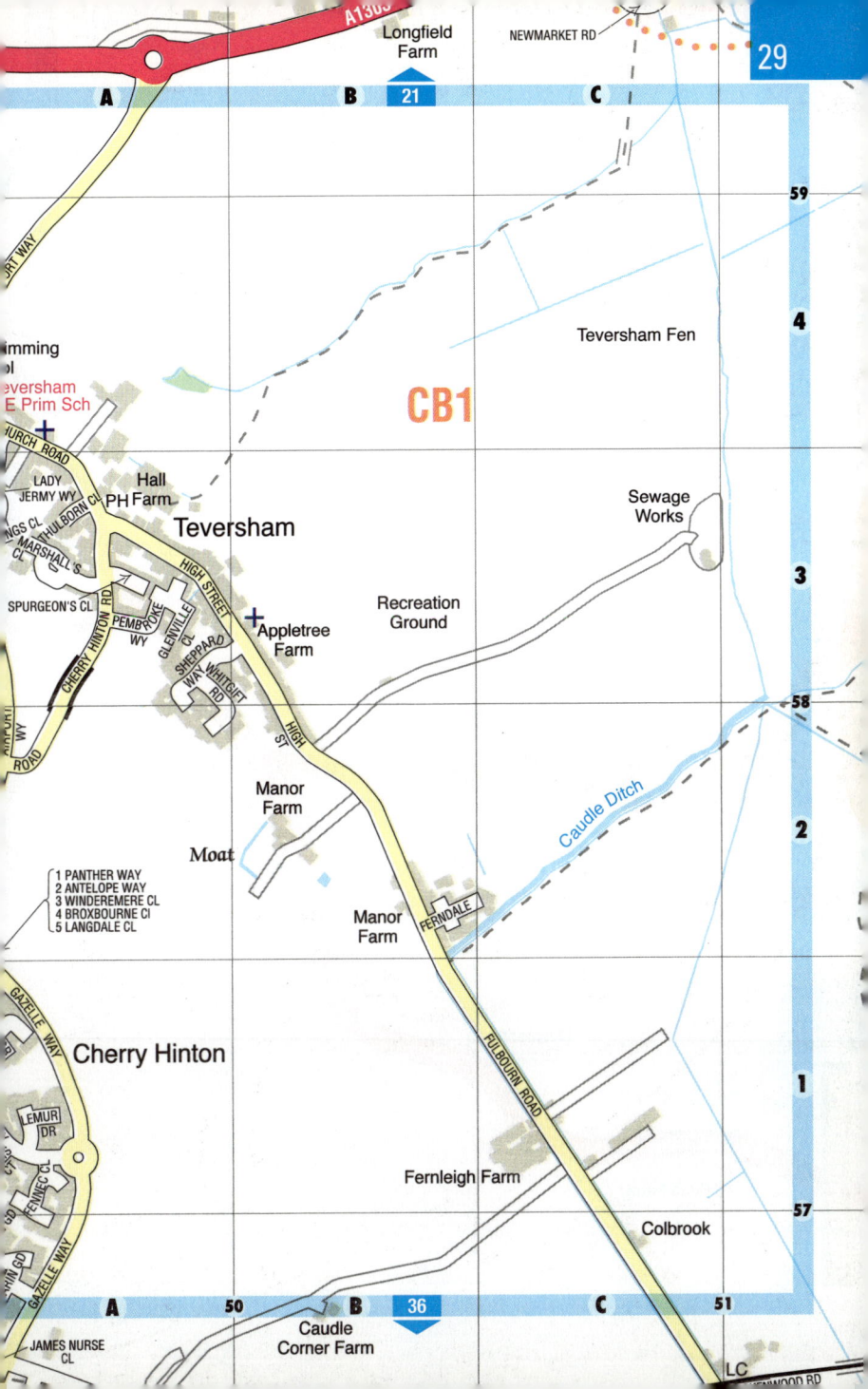

A1303
NEWMARKET RD
Longfield Farm
21

Teversham Fen

CB1

Teversham C E Prim Sch
CHURCH ROAD
LADY JERMY WY
Hall Farm
PH
Teversham
KINGS CL
MARSHALL'S
MULBERRY CL
SPURGEON'S CL
CHERRY HINTON RD
PEMBROKE WY
GLENVILLE CL
SHEPPARD WY
WHITGIFT RD
HIGH STREET
Appletree Farm

Sewage Works

Recreation Ground

HIGH ST
Manor Farm
Moat

1 PANTHER WAY
2 ANTELOPE WAY
3 WINDEREMERE CL
4 BROXBOURNE CL
5 LANGDALE CL

Manor Farm
FERNDALE

Caudle Ditch

Cherry Hinton
GAZELLE WAY
LEMUR DR
FENNEC CL

FULBOURN ROAD

Fernleigh Farm

Colbrook

50 **A** **B** **36** **C** **51**
JAMES NURSE CL
Caudle Corner Farm
LC
FENWOOD RD

59
4
3
58
2
1
57

23
A
B
C
GRANTCHESTER ROAD
57
4
3
56
2
1
55
Rifle Range
Haggis Farm
M11
12
Mast
CB3
Cemy
CAMBRIDGE ROAD
KINGS GROVE
HINES CL
PO
NEW ROAD
B1046
Moat
Barton CE
Prim Sch
SCHOOL LA
PH
CHURCH
LA
IVY
FIELD
ALLENS
CL
MAILES CL
MAILES
CL
GREAT CL
HIGH STREET
CAMBRIDGE RD
ROMAN HL
Barton
College
Farm
HOLBEN CL
HOLBEN CL
PH
Recreation
Ground
WIMPOLE ROAD A603
Birds Farm
HASLINGFIELD ROAD
A603 Royston (A1198)
41
Bourn Brook

FULBROO
BAR
A
B
24
C
Cambridge Rugby Football Ground
Pemb Colle Spo Grou
57
CB3
GRANTCHESTER ROAD
4
COTON ROAD
3
River Cam
32
56
BROADWAY
Grantchester
2
BRIDLE WAY
COTON RD
NUTTERS CL
PO
PH
TABRUM CL
STULP FIELD RD
BURNT CL
VICARAGE DR
HIGH STREET
HIGH ST
CROME DITCH CL
Moat
Rupert Brooke Museum
Manor Farm
MILL WAY
1
M11
55
Brasley Bridge
A
B
43
C
M11 Stansted Airport, London

32

CB3

Streets and Places

- FULBROOKE RD
- SELWYN RD
- Cambridge Rugby Football Ground
- Rugby Club
- Pembroke College Sports Ground
- St Catharine's College Sports Ground
- MILL
- HARDWICK ST
- MERTON ST
- CHEDWORTH ST
- Grove
- WEST VIEW
- ETBY AV
- GRANTCHESTER MDS
- SOUTH GN
- LOWER
- MILSTONE RD
- Newnham Croft Prim Sch
- B1:
  1. THE CENACLE
  2. NEWNHAM CFT ST
  3. GRANTCHESTER ST
  4. LAMMAS FIELD
- GRANTCHESTER ROAD
- River Cam
- LATHAM CL
- SO LATHA
- River Farm
- CH
- BROADWAY
- NUTT'S CL
- PH
- HIGH ST
- HIGH STREET
- Rupert Brooke Museum
- MILL WAY
- Eight Acre Wood
- Seven Acre Wood
- Trumpington Hall Park
- Trumpington Hall
- C1:
  1. LAMBOURN CL
  2. SOUTHBROOKE CL
  3. GAYTON CL
  4. BEVERLEY WY
- WYCHMORE DR
- A1309
- TRUMPINGTON HIGH ST
- A1134
- NORTH CTS
- GILMERTON CT
- GAZELEY RD
- WINGATE WAY
- WINGATE CL
- ALPHA TERRACE
- SEFTON CL
- MONKSWELL
- COSGROVNE ROAD
- MONKS
- PAGET ROAD
- Grantchester Road Plantation
- Brasley Bridge
- GRANTCHESTER ROAD
- CAMPBELL LA
- CHURCH LA
- Anstey Hall Farm
- MARIS LANE
- WHITLOCKS
- LINGREY CT
- ANSTEY WY
- ANSTEY WY
- CROSSWAYS GARDENS
- Anstey Hall
- BYR
- Tru

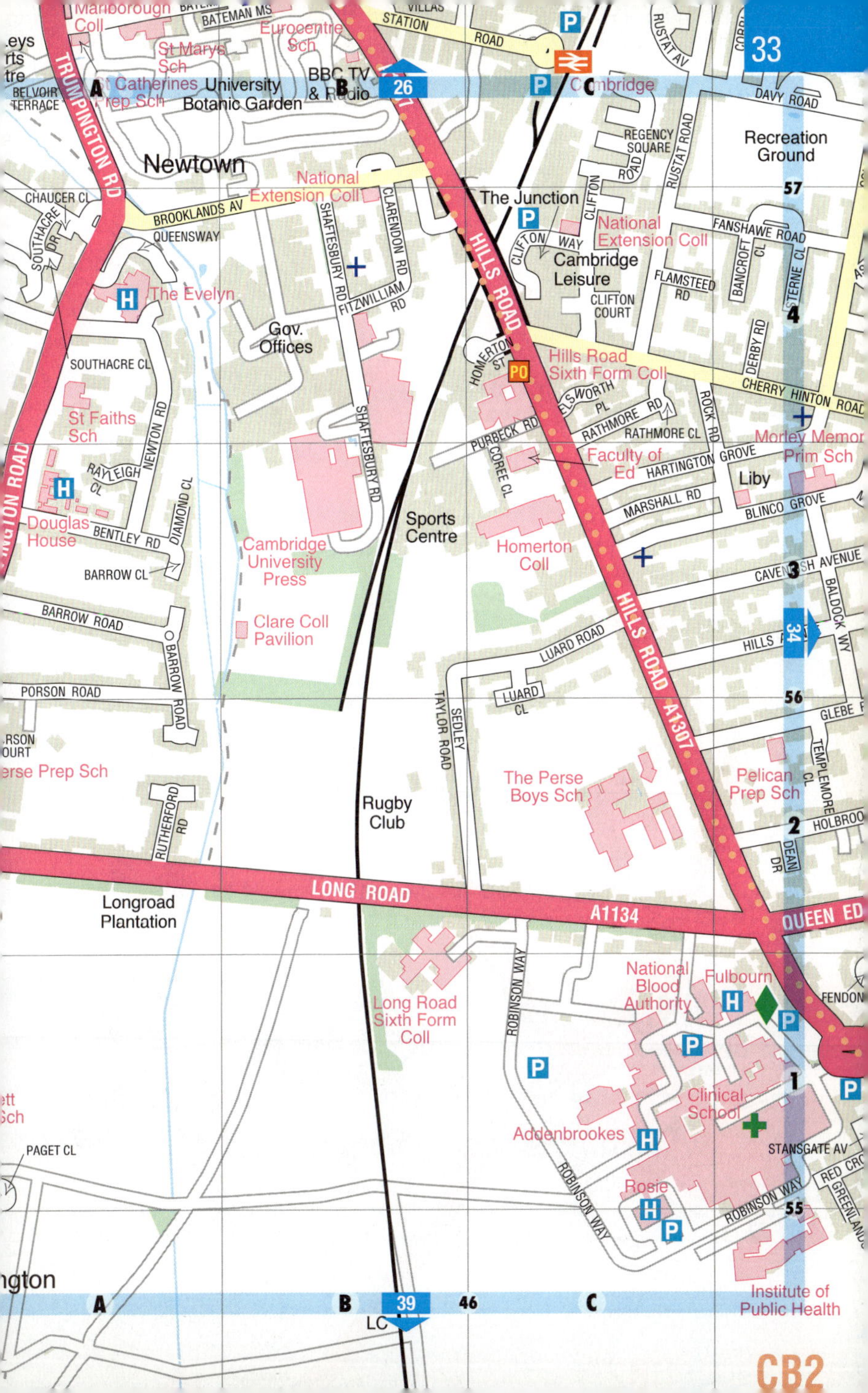
Marlborough Coll
BATEMAN MS
Eurocentre Sch
St Marys Sch
St Catherines Prep Sch
University Botanic Garden
BBC TV & Radio
26
STATION ROAD
Cambridge
RUSTAT AV
DAVY ROAD
TRUMPINGTON RD
BELVOIR TERRACE
A
B
C
Newtown
National Extension Coll
CHAUCER CL
SOUTHACRE DR
BROOKLANDS AV
QUEENSWAY
REGENCY SQUARE
RUSTAT ROAD
Recreation Ground
57
The Junction
CLIFTON WAY
CLIFTON RD
National Extension Coll
Cambridge Leisure
CLIFTON COURT
FANSHAWE ROAD
BANCROFT CL
STERNE CL
FLAMSTEED RD
SHAFTESBURY RD
CLARENDON RD
FITZWILLIAM RD
HILLS ROAD
The Evelyn
Gov. Offices
SOUTHACRE CL
HOMERTON ST
PO
Hills Road Sixth Form Coll
DERBY RD
4
CHERRY HINTON ROAD
ELSWORTH PL
RATHMORE RD
RATHMORE CL
ROCK RD
St Faiths Sch
PURBECK RD
COREE CL
Morley Memor Prim Sch
Faculty of Ed
HARTINGTON GROVE
Liby
RAYLEIGH CL
NEWTON RD
DIAMOND CL
MARSHALL RD
BLINCO GROVE
Douglas House
BENTLEY RD
Sports Centre
Homerton Coll
TRUMPINGTON ROAD
Cambridge University Press
BARROW CL
CAVENDISH AVENUE
3
BALDOCK WAY
BARROW ROAD
Clare Coll Pavilion
LUARD ROAD
34
HILLS ROAD A1307
HILLS AV
BARROW ROAD
LUARD CL
PORSON ROAD
SEDLEY TAYLOR ROAD
56
GLEBE RD
PERSE COURT
Perse Prep Sch
RUTHERFORD RD
The Perse Boys Sch
Pelican Prep Sch
TEMPLEMORE CL
Rugby Club
2
HOLBROOK
DEAN DR
LONG ROAD
A1134
QUEEN EDITH'S WAY
Longroad Plantation
National Blood Authority
Fulbourn
FENDON
Long Road Sixth Form Coll
ROBINSON WAY
Clinical School
1
Addenbrookes
STANSGATE AV
Rosie
RED CROSS
GREENLANDS
55
Institute of Public Health
PAGET CL
ngton
A
B
39
46
C
LC

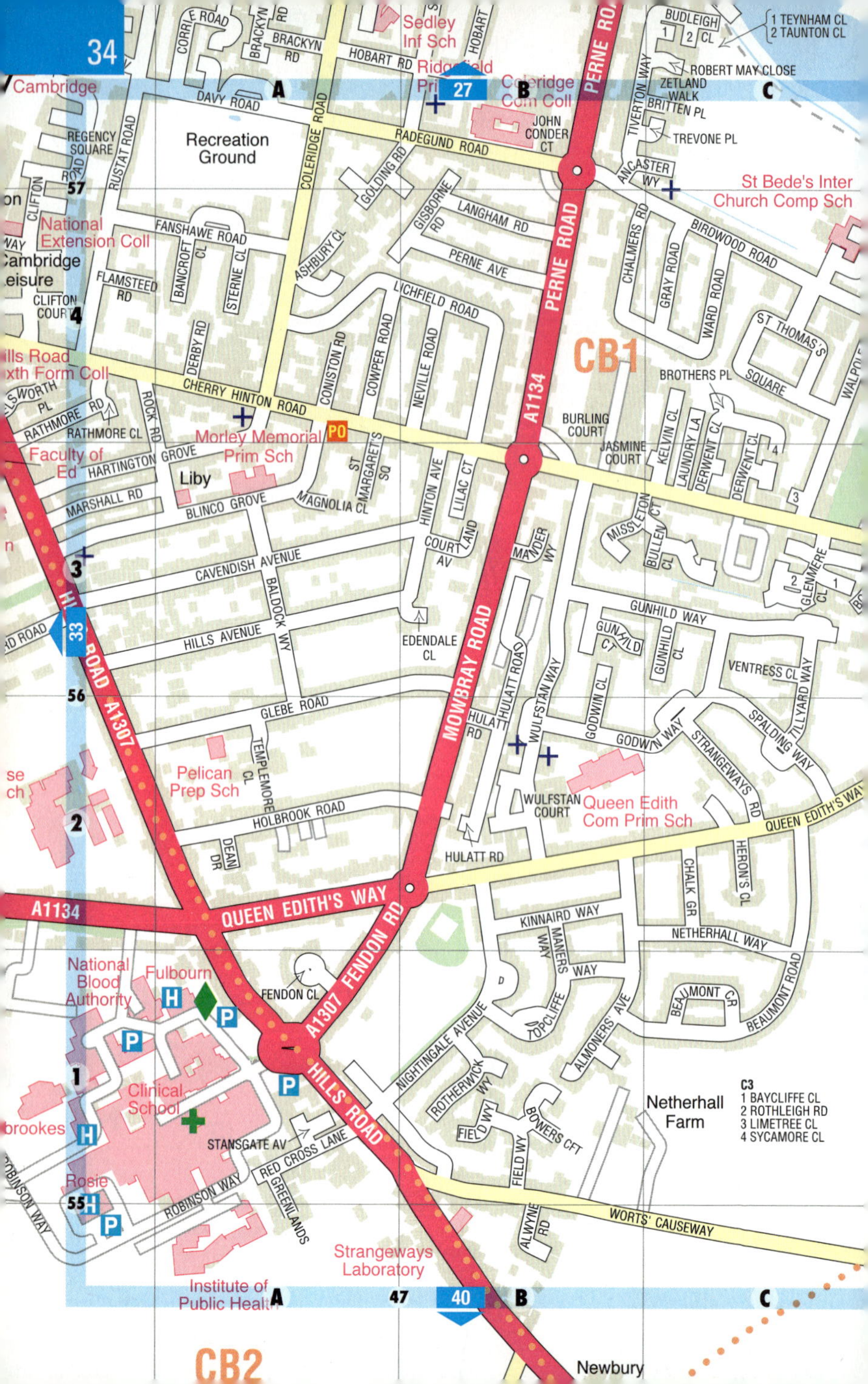
Cambridge
CORRIE ROAD
BRACKYN RD
BRACKYN RD
Sedley Inf Sch
HOBART RD
HOBART RD
Ridgefield Pri
27
Coleridge Com Coll
PERNE RD
BUDLEIGH CL
1 TEYNHAM CL
2 TAUNTON CL
ROBERT MAY CLOSE
ZETLAND WALK
BRITTEN PL
TIVERTON WAY
TREVONE PL
A
B
C
DAVY ROAD
REGENCY SQUARE
RUSTAT ROAD
Recreation Ground
COLERIDGE ROAD
RADEGUND ROAD
JOHN CONDER CT
ANCASTER WY
St Bede's Inter Church Comp Sch
57
CLIFTON ROAD
National Extension Coll
GOLDING RD
GISBORNE RD
LANGHAM RD
PERNE ROAD
CHALMERS RD
BIRDWOOD ROAD
FANSHAWE ROAD
BANCROFT CL
STERNE CL
ASHBURY CL
PERNE AVE
GRAY ROAD
WARD ROAD
Cambridge Leisure
FLAMSTEED RD
CLIFTON COURT
4
LICHFIELD ROAD
ST THOMAS'S SQUARE
DERBY RD
CONISTON RD
COWPER ROAD
NEVILLE ROAD
CB1
Hills Road Sixth Form Coll
CHERRY HINTON ROAD
A1134
BROTHERS PL
WALPOLE
RATHMORE RD
RATHMORE CL
ROCK RD
PO
BURLING COURT
JASMINE COURT
KELVIN CL
LAUNDRY LA
DERWENT CL
DERWENT CL
4
Morley Memorial Prim Sch
Faculty of Ed
HARTINGTON GROVE
Liby
ST MARGARET'S SQ
HINTON AVE
LILAC CT
3
MARSHALL RD
BLINCO GROVE
MAGNOLIA CL
MISSLETON CT
BULLEN CL
3
COURTLAND AV
MANDER WY
GLENMERE CL
2
1
CAVENDISH AVENUE
BALDOCK WAY
GUNHILD WAY
GUNHILD CT
GUNHILD CL
HILLS ROAD
33
HILLS AVENUE
EDENDALE CL
MOWBRAY ROAD
HULATT ROAD
WULFSTAN WAY
VENTRESS CL
TILLYARD WAY
56
A1307
GLEBE ROAD
HULATT RD
GODWIN CL
GODWIN WAY
STRANGEWAYS RD
SPALDING WAY
Pelican Prep Sch
TEMPLEMORE CL
WULFSTAN COURT
Queen Edith Com Prim Sch
QUEEN EDITH'S WAY
2
HOLBROOK ROAD
DEAN DR
HULATT RD
CHALK GR
HERON'S CL
A1134
QUEEN EDITH'S WAY
FENDON RD
KINNAIRD WAY
NETHERHALL WAY
MANERS WAY
National Blood Authority
Fulbourn
FENDON CL
A1307
TOPCLIFFE WAY
ALMONERS' AVE
BEAUMONT CR
BEAUMONT ROAD
1
NIGHTINGALE AVENUE
ROTHERWICK WY
HILLS ROAD
Clinical School
Netherhall Farm
C3
1 BAYCLIFFE CL
2 ROTHLEIGH RD
3 LIMETREE CL
4 SYCAMORE CL
Addenbrookes
STANSGATE AV
RED CROSS LANE
FIELD WY
BOWERS CFT
FIELD WY
ROBINSON WAY
Rosie
55
ROBINSON WAY
GREENLANDS
ALWYNE RD
WORTS' CAUSEWAY
Strangeways Laboratory
Institute of Public Health
A
47
40
B
C
CB2
Newbury

35

Cherry Hinton area map

Streets and places (labels visible on map):

- Kathleen Elliott Way
- Wolsey Way
- Newell Walk
- Queen's Meadow
- Neale Way
- Church End
- Teversham Drift
- Buffalo
- Madrill Cl
- Dolphin
- Capuchin Ct
- The Lynx
- Lemur Dr
- Loris Ct
- Fennec Cl
- Hayster Dr
- Railway St
- Orchard Est
- Fernlea Cl
- High St
- Kelsey Cr
- Leyburn Cl
- Sable Cl
- Roedeer Cl
- The Spinney Prim Sch
- Cherry Hinton CE Prim Sch
- Cherry Hinton Com Jun Sch
- LC
- Tenby Cl
- Bliss Cl
- Burnham Cl
- Fulbourn Old Drift
- Highdene Rd
- Tamarin Gd
- Gazelle Way
- Bede's Cr
- Bede's Gd
- Rickard Cl
- Haystar Dr
- Harcombe
- Doggett Rd
- Mill End Rd
- Crowthorne
- Claygate Rd
- Chartfield Rd
- Welstead Cl
- Sunmead Walk
- Lisle Walk
- Rush Gr
- Tamarin Gd
- James Nurse Cl
- Greystoke Ct
- Blenheim Cl
- Nacre Cl
- Sidney Farm Rd
- Chelwood Rd
- High Street
- Fisher's La
- Aran Cl
- Lucerne Cl
- Speedwell Cl
- LC
- Malvern Rd
- Wedgewood Dr
- Desmond Av
- Colville Road
- Pen Cl
- Shepherd's Cl
- Rose Cl
- Teasel Wy
- Bryan Ct
- Yarrow Road
- Superstore
- Cherry Hinton
- Liby
- Mill End
- Chequers Cl
- Colville Prim Sch
- Colville Rd
- Keates Rd
- Drayton Cl
- Bridewell Rd
- Violet Cl
- Clover Cl
- Annesley
- Cherry Hinton Road
- Forest
- Applewood Cl
- Headington Dr
- Leete Rd
- Drayton Rd
- Mallets Rd
- Colt's Foot
- Comfrey Ct
- Westgate
- Oake Cl
- Ventress Farm Ct
- Friar's Road
- Glads Way
- The Orchards
- PO
- Greystoke Rd
- Fulbourn Road
- Cambridge Rd
- Ainsdale
- Tweedale
- Peterhouse Technology Park
- The Netherhall Sch

B4
1 PAMPLIN CT
2 CHALFONT CL
3 CONWAY CL
4 AUGERS RD
5 DAWS CL

Cherry Hinton Close
Limekiln Close
Nature Reserve

Settlement
• Mast

Cherry Hinton
est Pit
e Reserve

Limekiln Road

Westbourn Farm

Bis F

Missleton Hill

Worts' Causeway
Worts' Causeway

Cherry Hinton

- Fernleigh Farm
- Colbro
- Cherry Hinton Com Jun Sch
- Caudle Corner Farm
- JAMES NURSE CL
- SPEEDWELL CL
- LC
- Superstore
- FULBOURN OLD DRIFT
- Ida Darwin H
- The Wind Sch
- Fulbourn H
- HINTON ROAD
- CB1
- CHER
- COMFREY
- CAMBRIDGE ROAD
- Fulbou Smock M
- Westbourn Farm
- SHELFORD ROAD
- Limepit Hill
- Bishop's Farm
- CAUSEWAY
- Mast

Streets: LEYBURN CT, ISABLE CL, ROEDEER CL, THE ELAND WY, LYNX, LEMUR DR, LORIS CL, FENNEC CL, BILSNHAM CL, FULBOURN OLD DRIFT, TAMARIN GD, GAZELLE WAY, HDGE LISLE WALK, RUSH, SPEEDWELL, YARROW ROAD, LUCERNE CL, ROSE CL, PRIM, TEASEL WY, ERIAN CT, VIOLET CL, CLOVER CT, BRINKWELL ROAD, ARBR CL, COLTSFOOT

A
B
C
Queens Farm
57
4
LC
ENWOOD RD
Barnbury Farm
COX'S DRO
HIGHFIELD GATE
APTHORPE ST
COW LANE
BRUNSWICK CT
HAM ROAD
STANSFIELD GD
GREATER FOXES
GREATER FOXES
STATION ROAD
NORTHFIELD
PIERCE LANE
THE MAPLES
BIRD FARM RD
WESTON GR
CARAWAY RD
HIGH ST
THE CHANTRY
CHURCH LA
Moat
3
THE HAVEN
THE CROFT
OSLAR'S WY
Fulbourn Prim Sch
PO
Fulbourne Manor
CHAPLIN'S CL
SWIFTS CR
HAGGIS GAP
ALL SAINTS RD
MANOR WALK
LUDLOW LA
MARCH'S CL
CARAWAY RD
WINDMILL LA
DUNMOWE WY
VIGOR'S RD
ST
SCHOOL LANE
56
FARMER'S ROW
GRANDRIDGE CL
HOLLMANS CL
Liby
THE BOURNS
GEOFFREY BISHOP AV
Mill Hill
HUNTSMILL
FROMONT CL
WRIGHTS GR
PETTITS CL
HOME END
STONEBRIDGE LANE
Fulbourn
DOGGET LA
IMPETT'S LANE
2
Highfield Farm
Cemy
BALSHAM RD
1
55
BABRAHAM ROAD
52
Grange Farm

38

Rupert Brooke Museum

Trumpington Hall Park

C1
1 LAMBOURN CL
2 SOUTHBROOKE CL
3 GAYTON CL
4 BEVERLEY WY

Trumpington 32

WINGATE CL
ALPHA TERRACE
SEFTON CL
MONKSWELL

A1309
SCOTSDOWNE ROAD
MONKSWELL
PAGET ROAD

Grantchester Road Plantation

CAMPBELL LA
CHURCH LA
WHITLOCKS
PO

Brasley Bridge

GRANTCHESTER ROAD
Anstey Hall Farm
LINGREY CT
MARIS LANE
ANSTEY WAY
PAGET RD

Anstey Hall
CROSSWAYS GARDENS
BYRON
Tru

Byron's Pool

Weir

Superstore

Cemy
THE BRAMBLES
ALLEN CT
CRAVEN CL
CRANLEIGH CL
LANTREE CR
LANTREE CR

HAUXTON ROAD
SHELFORD ROAD

P&R

BISHOP'S ROAD
BISHOP'S CT
EXETER CL

Glebe Farm

M11 (Huntingdon A14)
M11

HAUXTON ROAD
A1309

11

CAMBRIDGE ROAD
A10
M11

A10 Royston

M11 Stansted Airport, London

Hauxton

39

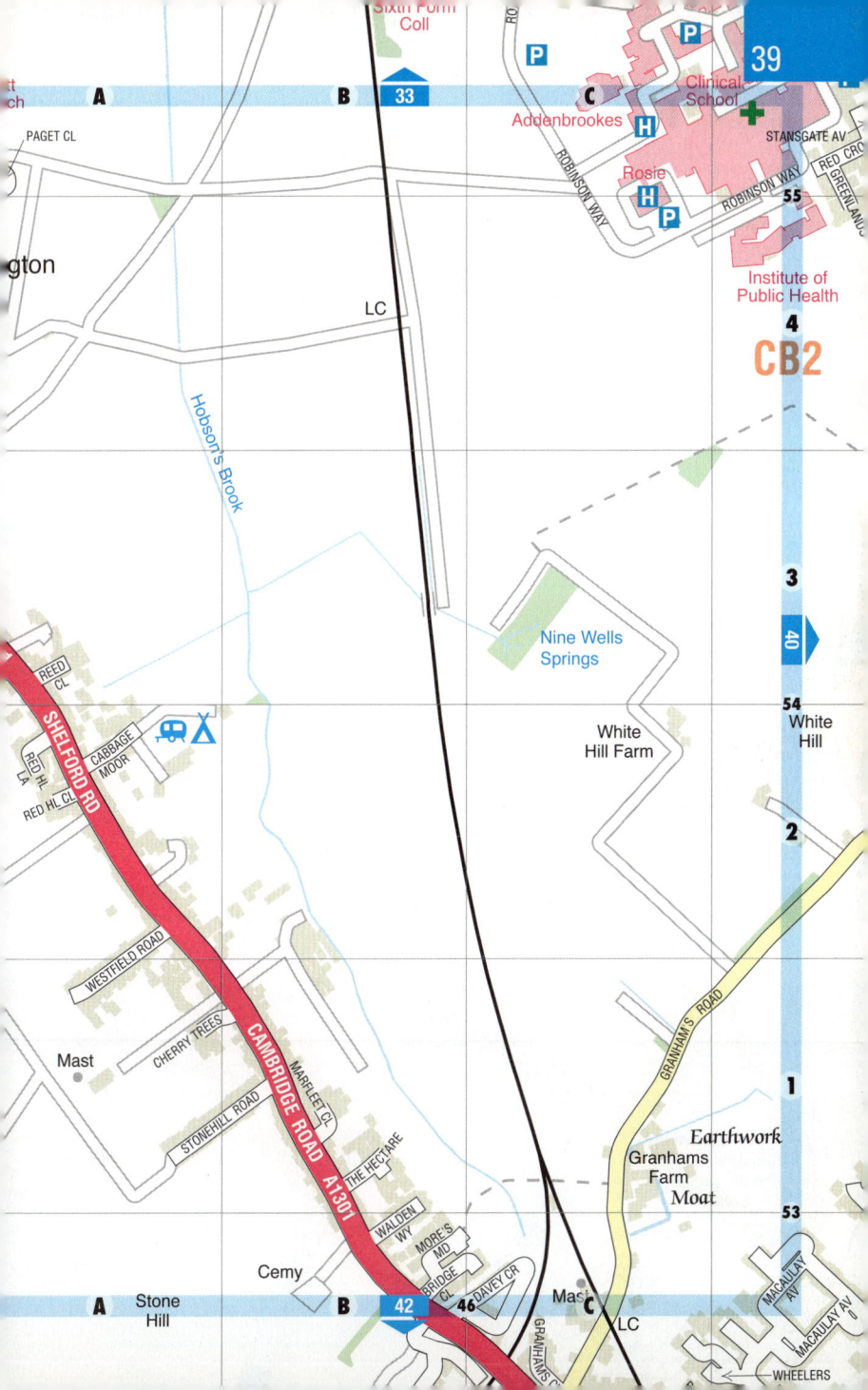

CB2

- Sixth Form Coll
- PAGET CL
- Addenbrookes
- Clinical School
- STANSGATE AV
- Rosie
- ROBINSON WAY
- RED CRO
- GREENLAN
- 55
- Institute of Public Health
- gton
- LC
- Hobson's Brook
- Nine Wells Springs
- 4
- 3
- 40
- 54 White Hill
- White Hill Farm
- REED CL
- RED HL CL
- RED HL LA
- SHELFORD RD
- CABBAGE MOOR
- WESTFIELD ROAD
- Mast
- CHERRY TREES
- STONEHILL ROAD
- MARFLEET CL
- CAMBRIDGE ROAD A1301
- THE HECTARE
- WALDEN WY
- MORE'S MD
- BRIDGE CL
- DAVEY CR
- Cemy
- Mast
- GRANHAM'S ROAD
- Earthwork
- Granhams Farm Moat
- MACAULAY AV
- 2
- 1
- 53
- Stone Hill
- 42
- 46
- LC
- WHEELERS
- A B 33 C
- A B 42 C

40

CB2

Locations and labels:
- Clinical School
- Addenbrooke's (brookes) H
- Stansgate Av
- Rosie H 55
- Robinson Way
- Red Cross Lane
- Greenlands
- Institute of Public Health
- Strangeways Laboratory
- Hill's Road / A130(?)
- Nightingale Avenue
- Field Wy
- Mowers Cft
- Alwyne Rd
- Almoners
- 70 Pol(?)
- Netherhall Farm
- Worts' Causeway
- Newbury Farm
- Babraham Road A1307
- Caius Farm
- P&R
- Hinton Wy
- White Hill Farm 54
- White Hill
- Clarke's Hill
- Granham's Road
- The Uplands
- Hillstead
- Granhams Farm 53
- Earthwork
- Moat
- Middlefield Farm
- Macaulay Av
- The Orchards
- Coppice Avenue
- Wheelers
- Mast LC

C3
1. RADCLIFFE CL
2. ROHLEIGH RD
3. LIMETREE CL
4. SYCAMORE CL

34 39 43 47 53 54 55

A B C

1 2 3 4

41

A — B — 35 — C

Missleton Hill

WORTS' CAUSEWAY

WORTS' CAUSEWAY

Beechwood Nature Reserve

CB2

BABRAHAM ROAD
A1307

Heath Farm

Wandlebury Country Park

Wandlebury

Fox Hill

Youth Wood

A1307

Long Plantation

Colin's Wood

Magog Down

Magog Wood

Wormwood Hill

Magog Wood

Memorial Wood

A1307 Haverhill

Little Trees Hill 49

Magog Down

Villedomer

55
4
3
54
2
1
53

A — B — C

42

A · B · C

Cherry Trees
Mast
Stonehill Road
Marlee Cl
39
Cambridge Road A1301
Granham
Granham Farm

The Hectare
Walden Wy
Cemy
More's Md
Bridge Cl
Davey Cr
Mast
LC

Stone Hill

Granham's Cl
De Frevil Rd

Maris Gn
PO
PH

Great Shelford
Tunwells Cl
Selwyn Cl
High Green
Poplar Cl
Shelford Av

Burlstead Rd
High Street
Elm's Av
Tunwells Lane
Ashen Gn
Liby
Woollards Lane
Spinney Dr
Crandal Wy

Manor Farm
Great & Little Shelford CE Prim Sch
Manor House
Church St
Peacocks
Woodland

LC
Hauxton Road
Manor Rd
Bridge Lane
Kings Mill La
Moat
Shelford Mill

Newton Road
PH
Church Street
Gd Fields
Little Shelford Recreation Ground

Beech Cl
PH
Courtyards

Little Shelford
High Street
Southcourts

Hall Farm

The Spinney
Whittlesford

45 · 46

43

CB2

Stapleford

- Hillstead
- Middlefield Farm
- Coppice Avenue
- Hinton Way
- Macaulay Av
- The Orchards
- Wheelers
- Orchard Rd
- Shelford
- Mingle Lane
- Cemy
- Dukes Md
- Gog Magog Way
- Hill Farm
- Haverhill Road
- Cleeway Av
- Headley Gdns
- Hawthorne Rd
- Granta Tr
- Dolphin Wy
- Priam's Wy
- Church Street
- Cox's Cl
- St Andrew's Cl
- Finch's Cl
- Bar Cl
- The Green Hedges Sch
- Moat
- Stapleford Com Prim Sch
- Bar La
- Aylesford Wy
- Heffer Cl
- Collier Wy
- Vine Wy
- Sternes Wy
- Forge End
- Anvil Cl
- Cherry Tree Av
- Greenfield Cl
- PH
- PO
- Bury Rd
- Poplar Wy
- Joscelynes
- Sawston Bridge
- Bury Farm
- London Road
- Cambridge Road
- Bentfield Lodge
- River Granta
- Cynamid Farm
- Dernford
- Barns Farm
- A1301 Saffron Walden (B184)

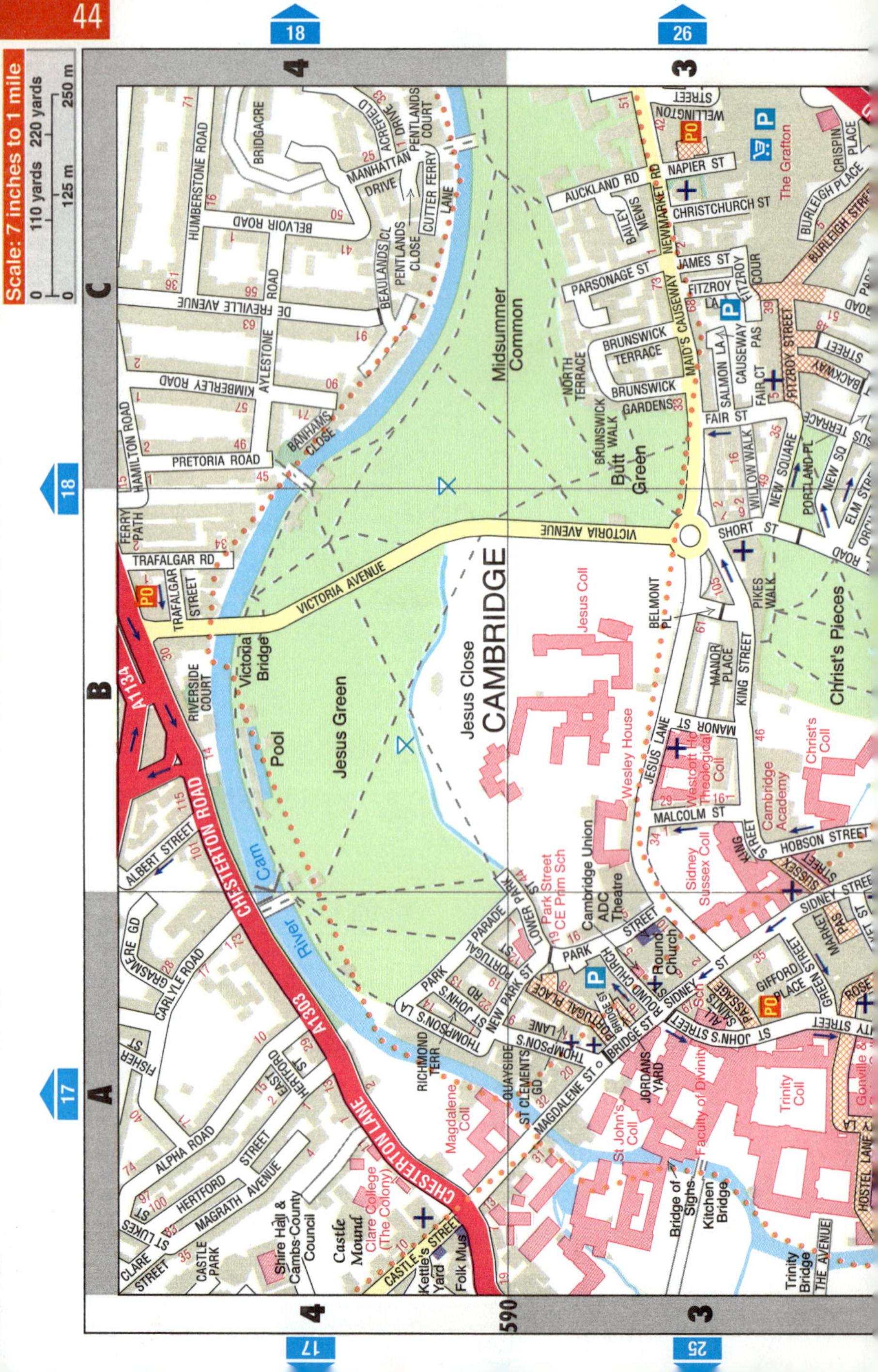
Scale: 7 inches to 1 mile
0 110 yards 220 yards
0 125 m 250 m
18
26
17
25
590
A
B
C
3
4
CAMBRIDGE
Jesus Green
Jesus Close
Midsummer Common
Butt Green
Christ's Pieces
Pool
River Cam
Victoria Bridge
VICTORIA AVENUE
CHESTERTON ROAD
A1134
A1303
CHESTERTON LANE
CASTLE STREET
Castle Mound
Shire Hall & Cambs County Council
Clare College (The Colony)
Kettle's Yard
Folk Mus
Magdalene Coll
St John's Coll
Trinity Coll
Jesus Coll
Christ's Coll
Sidney Sussex Coll
Westcott Ho Theological Coll
Wesley House
Cambridge Union
ADC Theatre
Round Church
Park Street CE Prim Sch
Faculty of Divinity
Cambridge Academy
Bridge of Sighs
Kitchen Bridge
Trinity Bridge
Gonville &
The Grafton
MAGDALENE ST
BRIDGE ST
ST JOHN'S STREET
SIDNEY ST
JESUS LANE
KING STREET
MALCOLM ST
MANOR PLACE
BELMONT PL
HOBSON STREET
PARK STREET
PARK PARADE
PORTUGAL PLACE
NEW PARK ST
THOMPSON'S LANE
QUAYSIDE
ST CLEMENTS GD
JORDANS YARD
ALL SAINTS PASSAGE
GIFFORD PLACE
GREEN STREET
MARKET PAS
SUSSEX STREET
NEWMARKET RD
MAID'S CAUSEWAY
FAIR ST
WILLOW WALK
NEW SQUARE
PORTLAND PL
SHORT ST
PIKES WALK
EMMANUEL ROAD
FITZROY STREET
BURLEIGH STREET
BURLEIGH PLACE
CRISPIN PLACE
NAPIER ST
AUCKLAND RD
CHRISTCHURCH ST
WELLINGTON STREET
PARSONAGE ST
JAMES ST
BRUNSWICK TERRACE
BRUNSWICK GARDENS
BRUNSWICK WALK
NORTH TERRACE
SALMON LA
CAUSEWAY PAS
FAIR CT
TRAFALGAR RD
TRAFALGAR STREET
RIVERSIDE COURT
FERRY PATH
HAMILTON ROAD
PRETORIA ROAD
KIMBERLEY ROAD
AYLESTONE ROAD
DE FREVILLE AVENUE
BELVOIR ROAD
HUMBERSTONE ROAD
BRIDGACRE
MANHATTAN DRIVE
ACREFIELD DRIVE
PENTLANDS COURT
PENTLANDS CLOSE
CUTTER FERRY LANE
BEAULANDS CL
BANHAMS CLOSE
ALBERT STREET
GRASMERE GD
CARLYLE ROAD
FISHER ST
ALPHA ROAD
HERTFORD STREET
EAST HERTFORD ST
MAGRATH AVENUE
ST LUKES STREET
CASTLE PARK
HOSTEL LANE
THE AVENUE
PO
P

45

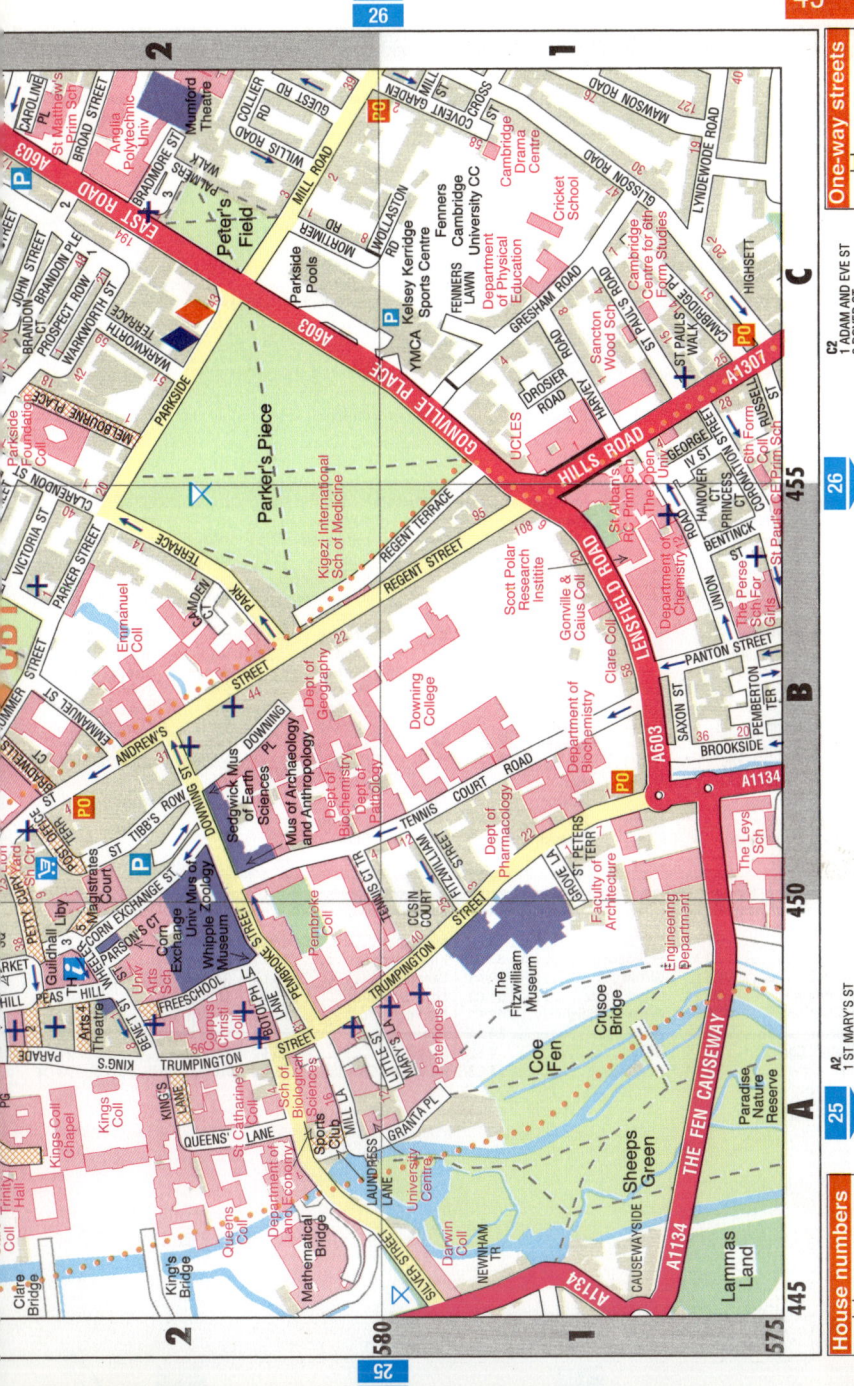

One-way streets

C2
1 ADAM AND EVE ST
2 DOVER ST
3 PETERSFIELD

A2
1 ST MARY'S ST
2 ST MARY'S PG
3 GUILDHALL ST
4 ST EDWARDS PG
5 GUILDHALL PL

House numbers
HIGH ST 1–59

Index

Street names are listed alphabetically and show the locality, the Postcode district, the page number and a reference to the square in which the name falls on the map page

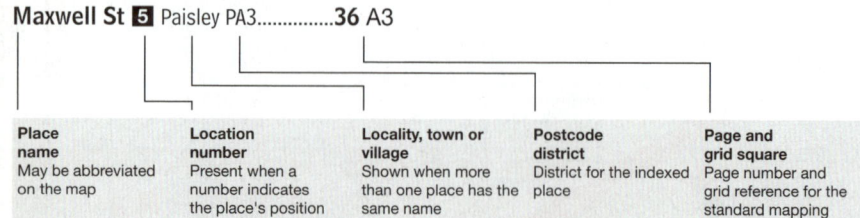

Maxwell St **5** Paisley PA3...............**36** A3

Place name	Location number	Locality, town or village	Postcode district	Page and grid square
May be abbreviated on the map	Present when a number indicates the place's position in a crowded area of mapping	Shown when more than one place has the same name	District for the indexed place	Page number and grid reference for the standard mapping

Public and commercial buildings are highlighted in magenta. **Places of interest** are highlighted in blue with a star★

Abbreviations used in the index

Acad	Academy	Ct	Court	Hts	Heights	Pl	Place
App	Approach	Ctr	Centre	Ind	Industrial	Prec	Precinct
Arc	Arcade	Ctry	Country	Inst	Institute	Prom	Prom
Ave	Avenue	Cty	County	Int	International	Rd	Road
Bglw	Bungalow	Dr	Drive	Intc	Interchange	Recn	Recreation
Bldg	Building	Dro	Drove	Junc	Junction	Ret	Retail
Bsns, Bus	Business	Ed	Education	L	Leisure	Sh	Shopping
Bvd	Boulevard	Emb	Embankment	La	Lane	Sq	Square
Cath	Cathedral	Est	Estate	Liby	Library	St	Street
Cir	Circus	Ex	Exhibition	Mdw	Meadow	Sta	Station
Cl	Close	Gd	Ground	Meml	Memorial	Terr	Terrace
Cnr	Corner	Gdn	Garden	Mkt	Market	TH	Town Hall
Coll	College	Gn	Green	Mus	Museum	Univ	University
Com	Community	Gr	Grove	Orch	Orchard	Wk, Wlk	Walk
Comm	Common	H	Hall	Pal	Palace	Wr	Water
Cott	Cottage	Ho	House	Par	Parade	Yd	Yard
Cres	Crescent	Hospl	Hospital	Pas	Passage		
Cswy	Causeway	HQ	Headquarters	Pk	Park		

Index of localities, towns and villages

Arbury............17 C4	Fen Ditton..........20 B3	Impington..........10 B4	Newtown...........26 A1
Barton............30 A1	Fulbourn............37 B2	Kings Hedges 11 A2	Oakington...........2 A3
Cambridge 25 C1	Girton...............9 A3	Landbeach 6 B4	Romsey Town 27 A2
Cambridge Airport ..28 B4	Grantchester.......31 C2	Little Shelford......42 A1	Stapleford.........43 C2
Cherry Hinton.......35 A3	Great Shelford 42 B3	Madingley..........14 A3	Stourbridge Common. 19 A2
Chesterton 18 C4	High Cross 24 A4	Milton..............13 A4	Stow cum Quy.......22 C4
Coldham's Common ..27 C4	Histon..............4 B2	Newnham 25 B2	Teversham 29 A3
Coton 23 A4	Horningsea.........13 C3	Newnham Croft......25 C1	Trumpington........38 C4

A

Abbey Meadows Primary School CB5 . . . . **27** C4
Abbey Road CB5 . . . . **18** C1
Abbey Street CB1 . . . . **26** C4
Abbey Walk CB1 . . . . **26** C4
Abbots Close CB4 . . . . **11** A1
Abbots Way CB5 . . . . **13** C3
Abercorn Place 6 CB4 **11** A2
Abrahams Close CB4 . . . . **6** C4
Acrefield Drive CB4 . . . . . **44** C4
Acton Way CB4 . . . . **17** C3
Adam and Eve Street 1
CB1 . . . . **45** C1
Adams Road CB3 . . . . **25** A4
ADC Theatre★ CB1 . . . . . **44** A3
Addenbrookes Hospital
CB2 . . . . **33** C1
Aingers Road CB4 . . . . . . **4** A2
Ainsdale CB1 . . . . **35** B3
Ainsworth Court 4
CB1 . . . . **26** C3
Ainsworth Place CB1 . . . **27** A3
Ainsworth Street CB1 . . **26** C3
Airport Way CB1 . . . . **29** A4
Akeman Street
Cambridge CB4 . . . . **17** B3
Landbeach CB4 . . . . **6** B4
Albemarle Way CB4 . . . . . **11** A1
Albert Road CB5 . . . . **22** C3
Albert Street CB4 . . . . **44** B4
Albion Row 6 CB3 . . . . . **17** B1
Albion Yard 5 CB3 . . . . . **17** B1
Alec Rolph Close CB1 . . **36** C3
Alex Wood Road CB4 . . **18** A4
All Saints Passage CB2 **44** A3
All Saints Road CB1 . . . . **37** B3
All Souls Lane CB3 . . . . . **17** A2
Allen Court CB2 . . . . **38** C4
Allens Close CB3 . . . . **30** A2
Almoners' Avenue CB1 **34** B1
Alpha Road CB4 . . . . **44** A1
Alpha Terrace CB2 . . . . . . **32** C1
Alstead Road CB4 . . . . . . **4** A3
Alwyne Road CB1 . . . . . . **40** B4
Ambrose Way CB4 . . . . . **4** B2
Amwell Road CB4 . . . . . . **11** B2
Ancaster Way CB1 . . . . . . **27** B1
Anglers Way CB4 . . . . **19** B3
Anglia Polytechnic Univ
CB1 . . . . **45** C2
Angus Close 2 CB1 . . . **26** C2
Annesley CB1 . . . . **35** A3
Ann's Road CB5 . . . . **20** A2
Anstey Way CB2 . . . . **38** C4
Antelope Way CB1 . . . . . . **28** C1
Anvil Close CB2 . . . . **43** B2
Apollo Way CB4 . . . . **11** A2
Applewood Close CB1 **35** B3
Apthorpe Street CB1 . . . **37** B4
Apthorpe Way CB4 . . . . . **11** C1
Aragon Close CB1 . . . . . . **11** A1
Arbury Court CB4 . . . . **18** A4
Arbury Primary School
CB4 . . . . **18** A3
Arbury Road CB4 . . . . **18** A4
Arcadia Gardens CB4 . . . **18** B3
Archway Court CB3 . . . . . **25** A1
Arden Road CB4 . . . . **11** B2
Argyle Street CB1 . . . . **27** A2
Armitage Way CB4 . . . . . . **11** B2
Arran Close CB1 . . . . **35** B4

Arthur Street CB4 . . . . . . **17** B2
Arts Theatre★ CB1 . . . . . **45** A3
Arundel Close CB4 . . . . . **17** B3
Ascham Road CB4 . . . . . . **18** A2
Ashbury Close CB1 . . . . . **34** A4
Ashcroft Court CB4 . . . . . **11** A1
Ashen Green CB2 . . . . **42** C3
Ashfield Road CB4 . . . . . . **19** A3
Ashley Court 9 CB1 . . . **26** C3
Ashvale CB1 . . . . **10** C1
Atherton Close CB4 . . . . . **18** A3
Athlone 7 CB1 . . . . **26** C3
Atkins Close CB1 . . . . **11** C1
Auckland Road CB5 . . . . **44** C3
Augers Road 4 CB1 . . **35** B4
Augustus Close 4 CB4 **11** A2
Australia Court CB3 . . . . **17** A2
Avenue The
Cambridge CB3 . . . . **44** A3
Girton CB3 . . . . **8** A3
Aylesborough Close 4
CB4 . . . . **10** C1
Aylesford Way CB2 . . . . . **43** A2
Aylestone Road CB4 . . . . **44** C4

B

Babraham Road
Cambridge CB2 . . . . **40** B1
Great Shelford CB2 . . . . . **41** A2
Badminton Close CB4 . . **17** B2
Bagot Place 5 CB4 . . . . **11** B2
Bailey Mews CB5 . . . . **44** C3
Bakery Close CB5 . . . . . . **20** A3
Baldock Way CB1 . . . . **34** A3
Ballard Close CB4 . . . . . . **6** C1
Bancroft Close CB1 . . . . . **34** A4
Bandon Road CB3 . . . . . . **16** B4
Banff Close 2 CB4 . . . . **11** A1
Banhams Close CB4 . . . . **44** C4
Banworth Lane CB4 . . . . **6** C4
Bar Close CB2 . . . . **43** B3
Bar Lane CB2 . . . . **43** B2
Barnabas Court CB4 . . . . **12** C3
Barnard Way 1 CB4 . . . **17** C3
Barnes Close CB5 . . . . . . **27** C4
Barnwell Drive CB1 . . . . . **28** A4
Barnwell Road CB1 . . . . . **27** C3
Barrow Close CB2 . . . . . . **33** A3
Barrow Road CB2 . . . . **33** A3
Barrowcrofts CB4 . . . . **4** A3
Barton CE Primary Sch
CB3 . . . . **30** A2
Barton Close CB3 . . . . **25** A2
Barton Road CB3 . . . . **25** A2
Basset Close 3 CB4 . . **11** B2
Bassett Close CB1 . . . . . . **11** B2
Bateman Mews CB2 . . . . **26** A1
Bateman Street CB2 . . . . **26** A1
Bateson Road CB4 . . . . . . **17** C2
Baycliffe Close 1 CB1 **34** C3
Bayford Place 1 CB4 . . **11** B2
Beaconsfield Terrace
CB4 . . . . **17** C2
Beales Way CB4 . . . . **11** C1
Beaulands Close CB4 . . . **44** C4
Beaumont Crescent
CB1 . . . . **34** C1
Beaumont Road CB1 . . . **34** C1
Beche Road CB5 . . . . **26** C4
Beech Close CB2 . . . . **42** A1
Beeches The CB4 . . . . **18** B3

Beechwood Nature Reserve★ CB1 . . . . **41** B4
Beehive Centre Retail Park
CB1 . . . . **27** C4
Belgrave Road CB1 . . . . . **27** B2
Bell Hill CB4 . . . . **4** A2
Belmont Place CB5 . . . . . **44** B3
Belmore Close 1 CB4 **17** B3
Belvoir Road CB4 . . . . **44** C4
Belvoir Terrace CB2 . . . . . **26** A1
Benet Close CB4 . . . . **12** B3
Bene't Street CB2 . . . . **45** A2
Benians Court CB3 . . . . . **17** A1
Benny's Way CB3 . . . . **23** A4
Benson Place 5 CB4 . . **17** B2
Benson Street 4 CB4 . . **17** B2
Bentinck Street CB2 . . . . **45** B1
Bentley Road CB2 . . . . . . **33** A3
Bergholt Close 4 CB5 **20** A2
Bermuda Road CB4 . . . . . **17** B2
Bermuda Terrace CB4 . . **17** B2
Beverley Way 4 CB2 . . **32** C1
Biggin Abbey★ CB5 . . . . **13** B2
Biggin Lane CB5 . . . . **13** B2
Birch Close CB4 . . . . **18** B3
Birch Trees Road CB2 . . **42** C4
Bird Farm Road CB1 . . . . **37** A3
Birdwood Road CB1 . . . . **34** C4
Bishop Way CB4 . . . . **4** B1
Bishop's Court CB2 . . . . . **38** B3
Bishop's Road CB2 . . . . . **38** C3
Blackhall Road CB3 . . . . . **10** B1
Blackthorn Close CB4 . . **18** B4
Blandford Close 1 CB4 **17** B4
Blanford Walk CB4 . . . . . . **10** B1
Blenheim Close 2 CB1 **35** A3
Blinco Grove CB1 . . . . **34** A3
Bliss Way CB1 . . . . **35** C4
Blossom Street 3 CB1 **26** C3
Borrowdale CB1 . . . . **17** B4
Bosworth Road CB4 . . . . **34** C3
Botolph Lane CB2 . . . . . . **45** A2
Bourne Road CB4 . . . . **19** B3
Bourns The CB1 . . . . **37** C2
Bowers Croft CB1 . . . . **34** B1
Brackenbury Close CB4 **4** B1
Brackley Close 3 CB4 **17** C4
Brackyn Road CB1 . . . . . . **27** A1
Bradmore Street CB1 . . **45** C2
Bradrushe Fields CB3 . . **16** B1
Bradwells Court CB1 . . . **45** B2
Brambles The
Cambridge CB2 . . . . **38** C4
Girton CB3 . . . . **16** C4
Bramley Court CB4 . . . . . **19** A4
Brampton Road CB1 . . . . **27** A3
Brandon Court CB1 . . . . . **45** C2
Brandon Place CB1 . . . . . **45** C2
Bray 6 CB1 . . . . **26** C3
Breckenham Road
CB1 . . . . **37** A4
Brentwood Close 6
CB5 . . . . **20** A2
Brentwood Court CB5 . . **20** A2
Bridewell Road CB1 . . . . **35** C3
Bridgacre CB1 . . . . **44** C1
Bridge Close CB2 . . . . **42** B4
Bridge Lane CB2 . . . . **42** A2
Bridge of Sighs★ CB3 . . **44** A3
Bridge Road Histon CB4 **10** B4
Impington CB4 . . . . **10** B2
Bridge Street CB2 . . . . . . **44** A3
Bridle Way CB3 . . . . **31** B2

Abb – Cam 47

Brierley Walk CB4 . . . . **10** B1
Brimley Road CB4 . . . . . . **17** C4
Britannic Way CB1 . . . . . . **28** B1
British Antarctic Survey
CB3 . . . . **16** A1
Britten Place CB1 . . . . **27** C1
Broad Street CB1 . . . . **45** C2
Broadway CB3 . . . . **31** C2
Broadway The
Oakington/Longstanton CB4 **2** A3
Romsey Town CB1 . . . . . . **27** A2
Brook Close CB4 . . . . **4** A2
Brook Lane CB3 . . . . **23** B4
Brookfield Road CB3 . . . **23** A4
Brookfields CB1 . . . . **27** C1
Brookfields Hospital
CB1 . . . . **27** B2
Brooklands Avenue
CB2 . . . . **33** A4
Brooks Road CB1 . . . . **27** C2
Brookside CB2 . . . . **45** B1
Brookside Lane 1 CB2 **26** C1
Brothers Place CB4 . . . . . **34** C4
Broughton House Gallery★
CB1 . . . . **44** B3
Brownlow Road CB4 . . . **17** B4
Broxbourne Close CB1 **28** C1
Brunswick Court CB1 . . **37** A3
Brunswick Gardens
CB5 . . . . **44** C3
Brunswick Terrace CB5 **44** C3
Brunswick Walk CB1 . . . **44** C3
Buchan Street CB4 . . . . . **11** A1
Buckingham Road CB3 **17** B1
Budleigh Close CB1 . . . . **27** C1
Buffalo Way CB1 . . . . **28** C1
Bullard Laboratories
CB3 . . . . **16** C2
Bullen Close CB1 . . . . **34** C3
Bulstrode Gardens CB3 **24** C4
Bulteel Close CB4 . . . . . . **6** B1
Burgoynes Farm Close
CB4 . . . . **4** C1
Burgoyne's Road CB4 . . **4** C1
Buristead Road CB2 . . . . **42** B3
Burkett Way CB4 . . . . **4** A3
Burleigh Place CB1 . . . . . **44** C3
Burleigh Street CB1 . . . . **44** C3
Burling Court CB1 . . . . . . **34** B4
Burling Walk CB4 . . . . **6** C1
Burnham Close CB1 . . . . **35** C4
Burnside CB1 . . . . **27** C1
Burnt Close CB3 . . . . **31** C2
Burrough Field CB4 . . . . **10** B3
Bury Road CB2 . . . . **43** B2
Butcher Close CB4 . . . . . **6** B1
Butler Way CB4 . . . . **17** C4
Butt Lane CB4 . . . . **6** A1
Byron Square CB2 . . . . . . **38** C4

C

Cabbage Moor CB2 . . . . . **39** A2
Cadwin Field CB4 . . . . . . **11** B1
Caithness Court CB4 . . . **11** A2
Caledon Way 3 CB4 . . **11** A2
Callander Close CB1 . . . . **10** C1
Cam Causeway CB1 . . . . **19** A4
Cambanks CB1 . . . . **18** C2
Cambridge & County Folk Museum★ CB3 . . . . **44** A4

48 Cam – Dan

Cambridge Academy
CB1 .... **44** B3
Cambridge Airport CB1 **28** B4
Cambridge Business Park
CB4 .... **12** B2
Cambridge Centre For Sixth Form Studies CB1 ... **17** B2
Cambridge Drama Centre
CB1 .... **45** C1
Cambridge Leisure
CB1 .... **33** C6
Cambridge Place CB1 ..**45** C1
Cambridge Road
Fulbourn CB1 .... **35** C3
Girton CB3 .... **9** A2
Great Shelford CB2 ...**39** B1
Histon CB4 ....**10** B2
Madingley CB3 ....**14** B3
Milton CB4 ....**12** B3
Oakington/Longstanton CB4 **2** B2
Cambridge Regional College CB4 ....**11** B2
Cambridge Retail Park
CB5 .... **19** A1
Cambridge Science Park
CB4 .... **12** A2
Cambridge Sta CB1 ....**26** C1
Cambridge Summer Sch of Technology CB3 ....**25** A1
Cambridge University Botanic Garden★ CB2 **26** B1
Cambridge University Centre CB2 ....**45** A1
Cambridge University Press
CB2 .... **33** B3
Camden Court CB1 ....**45** B2
Cameron Road CB4 ....**11** A1
Campbell Lane CB2 ....**38** B4
Campbell Street 1
CB1 .... **27** A2
Campkin Court CB4 ....**11** B1
Campkin Road CB4 ....**11** B1
Camside CB4 ....**18** C2
Canterbury Close CB4 ..**17** B2
Canterbury Street CB4 .**17** B2
Capstan Close CB4 .....**18** C1
Capuchin Court CB1 ..**28** C1
Car Dyke Road
Landbeach CB5 ....**7** B4
Waterbeach CB5 ....**7** C4
Caravere Close 2 CB4 **11** B2
Caraway Road CB1 ....**37** A3
Caribou Way CB1 ......**28** C1
Carisbrooke Road CB4 .**17** B3
Carlow 9 CB1 ....**26** C4
Carlton Way CB4 ......**17** C3
Carlyle Road CB4 ......**44** A4
Caroline Place CB1 ....**45** C2
Carrick Close CB1 .....**35** A3
Castle Hill Gallery★
CB4 .... **17** B2
Castle Park CB1 ....**44** A4
Castle Row 8 CB3 ....**17** B1
Castle Street CB3 .....**44** A4
Catharine Street CB1 ..**27** A2
Causeway Passage CB1 **44** C2
Causewayside CB1 ....**45** A1
Cavendish Avenue CB1 **34** A3
Cavendish Road CB1 ..**27** A3
Cavesson Court CB4 ..**17** B2
Cenacle The 1 CB3 ...**25** B1

Centre For Mathematical Sciences CB3 ....**25** A4
Chalfont Close 2 CB1 .**35** B4
Chalk Grove CB1 ......**34** C2
Chalmers Road CB1 ....**34** B4
Champneys Walk CB3 .**25** B2
Chancellors Walk 2
CB4 .... **17** B4
Chantry Close CB4 ....**18** B2
Chantry The CB1 ......**37** C3
Chapel Street CB4 .....**18** C2
Chaplin's Close CB1 ...**37** B3
Chapman Court CB4 ..**11** A1
Charles Street CB1 ....**27** A1
Chartfield Road CB1 ...**35** B4
Chaston Road CB2 ....**42** C3
Chatsworth Avenue
CB4 .... **17** B3
Chaucer Close CB2 ....**33** A4
Chaucer Road CB2 ....**25** C1
Cheddars Lane CB5 ...**19** A1
Chedworth Street CB3 .**25** B1
Chelwood Road CB1 ..**35** B4
Cheney Way CB4 ......**19** B3
Chequers Close CB1 ..**35** B3
Chequers Road CB4 ..**10** B4
Cherry Bounds Road
CB3 .... **9** A2
Cherry Close
Cambridge CB1 ....**35** A3
Milton CB4 ....**6** C1
Cherry Hinton CE Inf Sch
CB1 .... **35** B4
Cherry Hinton Close Limekiln Close Nature Reserve★ CB1 .....**35** B2
Cherry Hinton Com Jun Sch
CB1 .... **35** C4
Cherry Hinton Road
Cambridge CB1 ....**34** A4
Great Shelford CB2 ...**40** C3
Teversham CB1 ....**28** C2
Cherry Hinton West Pit Nature Reserve★ CB1 .**35** A2
Cherry Orchard
Fulbourn CB1 ....**36** C3
Oakington/Longstanton CB4 **2** B3
Cherry Tree Avenue
CB2 .... **43** B2
Cherry Trees CB2 ......**39** A1
Cherwell Court CB3 ...**25** B1
Chesnut Grove CB4 ...**18** B2
Chesterfield Road CB4 .**18** C4
Chesterton Community College CB4 ....**18** A2
Chesterton Hall Crescent
CB4 .... **18** B2
Chesterton Hospital
CB4 .... **18** B2
Chesterton Lane CB4 ..**44** A4
Chesterton Road CB4 ..**44** A4
Chestnut Grove CB4 ..**18** B2
Chigwell Court 7 CB5 .**20** A2
Chivers Way CB4 .....**10** A4
Christchurch Street
CB1 .... **44** C3
Christ's Coll CB1 ......**44** B3
Church End
Cambridge CB1 ....**28** B2
Coton CB3 ....**23** A4
Horningsea CB5 ....**13** C4
Church Lane Barton CB3 **30** A2
Cambridge CB2 ....**38** B4

Church Lane continued
Fulbourn CB1 ....**37** C3
Girton CB3 ....**9** A2
Madingley CB3 ....**14** A2
Milton CB4 ....**12** C4
Church Rate Walk CB3 **25** B2
Church Road
Stow cum Quy CB5 ....**22** B2
Teversham CB1 ....**29** A4
Church Street
Cambridge CB4 ....**18** C2
Fen Ditton CB5 ....**20** A4
Great Shelford CB2 ...**42** A2
Stapleford CB2 ....**43** B2
Histon CB4 ....**4** B3
Church View CB4 ......**2** B4
Churchfield Court CB3 ..**9** A4
Churchill College CB3 ..**17** A1
City Road CB1 ....**45** C2
Clare College (The Colony)
CB4 .... **44** A4
Clare Coll CB2 ....**45** A2
Clare Coll Pavilion CB2 **33** B3
Clare Road CB3 ....**25** B2
Clare Street CB4 ......**44** A4
Claremont 1 CB1 ....**26** B1
Clarendon Road CB2 ..**33** B4
Clarendon Street CB1 ..**45** B2
Clarkson Close CB3 ...**25** A4
Clarkson Road CB3 ...**25** A4
Clay Close Lane CB4 ...**4** C1
Clay Street CB4 ....**4** A3
Claygate Road CB1 ...**35** B4
Clerk Maxwell Road
CB3 .... **24** C4
Clifton Court CB1 .....**33** C4
Clifton Road CB1 .....**33** C4
Clifton Way CB1 ......**33** C4
Cliveden Close CB4 ...**17** B3
Clover Court CB1 ......**35** C3
Cobble Yard CB1 ......**44** C3
Cobholm Place 4 CB4 **11** B2
Cockburn Street CB1 ..**27** A2
Cockcroft Place CB3 ...**25** A4
Cockerell Road CB4 ...**17** C3
Cockerton Road CB3 ...**9** A3
Coggeshall Close 5
CB5 .... **20** A2
Colbrook CB1 ....**36** C4
Coldham's Grove CB1 .**27** B3
Coldham's Lane CB1 ..**27** B4
Coldham's Road CB1 ..**27** A4
Coleridge Com Coll
CB1 .... **27** B1
Coleridge Road CB1 ..**34** A4
Coles Lane CB4 ....**2** B4
Coles Road CB4 ....**12** C4
Coll of West Anglia CB4 **6** C1
College Fields CB4 .....**18** B4
College Road CB4 .....**10** A3
Collier Road CB1 ......**45** C2
Collier Way CB2 ......**43** B2
Colliers Lane CB5 .....**22** C4
Coltsfoot Close CB1 ...**35** C3
Colville Prim Sch CB1 .**35** B3
Colville Road CB1 .....**35** B4
Colwyn Close CB4 ....**17** C3
Comfrey Court CB1 ...**35** C3
Computer Laboratory
CB3 .... **16** C1
Conder Close CB4 ......**6** B1
Conduit Head Road
CB3 .... **16** B1

Coniston Road CB1 ....**34** A4
Consul Court 8 CB4 ..**11** A1
Conway Close 3 CB1 .**35** B4
Cook Close CB4 ....**19** A4
Coppice Avenue CB2 ..**43** A4
Coppice The CB4 ......**10** B3
Coral Park Trading Estate
CB1 .... **27** A4
Coree Close CB2 ......**33** A4
Corn Exchange★ CB1 .**45** A2
Corn Exchange Street
CB2 .... **45** A2
Corona Road CB4 .....**18** A2
Coronation Mews 2
CB2 .... **26** A1
Coronation Place CB2 .**26** A1
Coronation Street CB2 .**45** B1
Corpus Christi Coll CB2 **45** A2
Corrie Road CB1 ......**27** A1
Cosin Court CB1 ......**45** A1
Coton CE Primary School
CB3 .... **23** A4
Coton Road CB3 ......**31** A3
Cottenham Road CB4 ..**4** A3
Coulson Close CB4 ....**12** B4
Courtland Avenue CB1 .**34** B3
Courtney Way CB4 ...**18** A2
Courtyards CB2 ....**42** B1
Covent Garden CB1 ...**45** C1
Cow Lane CB1 ....**37** A3
Cowley Park CB4 .....**12** A1
Cowley Road CB4 .....**12** B1
Cowper Road CB1 ....**34** A4
Cox's Close CB2 ......**43** B2
Cox's Drove CB1 ......**37** B4
Craister Court CB4 ....**11** A1
Crandal Way CB2 .....**42** C2
Cranleigh Close CB2 ...**38** C3
Cranmer Road CB3 ...**25** A3
Crathern Way CB4 ....**11** B1
Crathern Way CB4 ....**11** B1
Craven Close CB2 .....**38** C4
Crescent Road CB4 ...**10** B3
Crescent The
Cambridge CB3 ....**17** A1
Impington CB4 ....**10** B3
Cricket School CB1 ....**45** C1
Crispin Close 1 CB4 ..**10** C1
Crispin Place CB1 .....**44** C3
Croft Close CB4 ....**4** A3
Croft Gardens CB3 ....**25** B1
Croft Lane CB4 ....**2** A4
Croft The CB1 ....**37** A3
Croftgate CB3 ....**24** C1
Crome Ditch Close CB3 **31** C2
Cromwell Road CB1 ...**27** A3
Crosfield Court CB4 ...**11** A1
Cross Street CB1 ......**45** C1
Crossways Gardens
CB2 .... **38** C4
Crowland Way CB4 ...**11** B1
Crowthorne Close CB1 **35** B4
Cunningham Close CB4 **18** A4
Cutter Ferry Close CB4 **18** C1
Cutter Ferry Lane CB4 .**44** C4
Cyprus Road CB1 .....**27** B1

D

Daisy Close CB4 ......**10** C1
Dalegarth CB4 ....**18** B2
Dalton Square CB4 ....**19** A3
Dane Drive CB3 ....**24** C3

Danesbury Court CB1 ..27 B3	Edwinstowe Close CB2 33 A4	Fison Road CB5 ....20 A2	**Dan – Gre** 49
Darwin Coll CB3 ......45 A1	Egerton Close CB5 ....19 A2	Fitzroy Court CB1 .....44 C3	
Darwin Drive CB4 .....17 C3	Egerton Road CB5 ....20 A2	Fitzroy Lane CB5 ......44 C3	Gifford's Close CB3 ....9 A2
Davey Close CB4 ....4 B1	Ekin Road CB5 ....19 C2	Fitzroy Street CB1 ....44 C3	Gilbert Close CB4 .....17 B3
Davey Crescent CB2 ...42 C4	Ekin Walk CB5 ....19 C1	**Fitzwilliam College**	Gilbert Road CB4 .....17 C3
David Bull Way CB4 .....6 C1	Eland Way CB1 ....28 C1	CB3 ....17 A2	Gilmerton Court CB2 ...32 C2
David Street 5 CB1 ...26 C2	Elder Close CB4 ......18 B4	**Fitzwilliam Museum The★**	**Girton College**
Davy Road CB1 ....27 A1	Elfleda Road CB5 .....19 B1	CB2 ....45 A1	Cambridge CB3 ....25 A4
Daws Close 5 CB1 ...35 B4	Elizabeth Way CB4 ....18 B2	Fitzwilliam Road CB2 ..33 B3	Girton CB3 ....16 B4
De Freville Avenue CB4 44 C4	Ellesmere Road CB4 ...17 C4	Fitzwilliam Street CB2 .45 B1	**Girton Glebe Prim Sch**
De Freville Road CB2 ..42 C4	Ellison Close CB4 .....10 C1	Flamsteed Road CB1 ...33 C4	CB3 ....9 A3
Dean Drive CB1 ....34 A2	Elm Street CB1 ....44 B3	**Fletcher's Way** 3	Girton Road CB3 ....9 B1
Dennis Road CB5 .....20 B2	Elmfield Road CB4 ....18 C3	CB1 ....26 C2	Gisborne Road CB1 ...34 B4
Dennis Wilson Court	Elm's Avenue CB2 ....42 C3	Flower Street 2 CB1 .26 C2	Gladstone Way CB1 ...35 B3
CB2 ....32 C2	Elms The CB4 ....12 B4	**Folk Museum★** CB1 ..44 B4	Glebe Road CB1 ......34 A2
Derby Road CB1 ......34 A4	Elsworth Place CB1 ...33 C4	Fontwell Avenue CB4 ..17 B3	Glebe Way CB4 ....4 B2
Derby Street CB3 .....25 B1	Eltisley Avenue CB3 ...25 B1	Footpath The CB3 ....23 B4	Glenacre Close 3 CB1 35 A3
Derwent Close CB1 ...34 C3	Ely Road CB5 ....7 A1	Fordwich Close 1 CB4 17 C4	Glenmere Close CB1 ..34 C3
Desmond Avenue CB1 .35 B4	Emery Road CB1 .....26 C3	Forest Road CB1 .....35 A3	Glenville Close CB1 ...29 A3
Devonshire Road CB1 .26 C2	Emery Street CB1 ....26 C2	Forge End CB2 ....43 B2	Glisson Road CB1 ....45 C1
Diamond Close CB2 ...33 A3	**Emmanuel Coll** CB1 ..45 B2	Fortescue Road CB4 ..18 A4	Godesdone Road CB5 ..18 C1
Ditchburn Place CB1 ..26 C3	Emmanuel Road CB1 ..45 B2	Forum Court 7 CB4 ..11 A1	Goding Way CB4 ......13 A2
Ditton Fields CB5 .....19 B1	Emmanuel Street CB1 .45 B2	Foster Road CB1 .....38 C4	Godwin Close CB1 ...34 B2
Ditton Lane CB5 .....20 A2	Emperor Court 8 CB4 .11 A2	Fox's Close CB4 ......12 C4	Godwin Way CB1 ....34 B2
Ditton Walk CB5 .....19 B2	Enfield 8 CB1 ....26 C4	**Francis Darwin Court**	Gog Magog Way CB2 ..43 B3
Dock Lane CB5 ....13 C4	Ennisdale Close 9 CB1 19 A1	CB4 ....17 B3	Golding Road CB1 ....34 B4
Doctor's Close CB4 ....4 C1	Enniskillen Road CB4 ..19 A3	**Francis Passage** 3	**Gonville & Caius Coll**
Dodford Lane CB3 .....9 A4	Erasmus Close CB4 ...17 C3	CB2 ....26 A1	CB2 ....45 B1
Dogget Lane CB1 .....37 B2	Essex Close CB4 .....18 A3	Frank's Lane CB1 ....19 A3	Gonville Place CB1 ....45 C1
Doggett Road CB1 ...35 A4	Eurocentre Sch CB2 ...26 B1	Fraser Road CB4 .....18 C4	Gough Way CB3 .....24 C2
Dole The CB4 ....4 B1	**Evelyn Hospital The**	Free School Lane CB2 .45 A2	Gowers The CB3 ....9 A3
Dolphin Close CB1 ...28 C1	CB2 ....33 A4	French's Road CB4 ...17 C2	**Grace Sch of Medicine**
Dolphin Way CB2 ....43 A2	Evergreens CB4 ......19 A3	Friar's Close CB1 .....35 B3	CB2 ....26 C2
Donegal 7 CB1 ......26 C4	Exeter Close CB2 .....38 C3	Froment Way CB4 .....6 B1	Grafton Centre CB1 ..44 B3
Douglas House Hospital		Fromont Close CB1 ...37 A2	Grafton Street CB1 ...45 C2
CB2 ....33 A3	**F**	**Fulbourn Hospital**	Grain Close CB2 .....42 C3
Dover Street 2 CB1 ..45 C2		Cambridge CB2 ....34 A1	Grandridge Close CB1 .37 B2
Dowding Way CB4 ...17 C4	Fair Court CB1 ....44 C3	Fulbourn CB1 ....36 B3	Grange Court CB3 ....25 A2
Downham's Lane CB4 .18 C4	Fair Street CB1 ....44 C3	Fulbourn Old Drift CB5 35 C4	Grange Drive CB3 .....9 A1
Downing Coll CB2 ...45 B1	Fairbairn Road CB4 ..19 B3	**Fulbourn Primary Sch**	Grange Road CB3 ....25 A2
Downing Place CB2 ...45 B2	Fairfax Road CB1 ....27 A3	CB1 ....37 B3	**Granham's Road**
Downing Street CB2 ..45 B2	Fairway CB3 ....9 A4	**Fulbourn Road**	Cambridge CB2 ....40 B3
Drake Way CB4 ....4 B3	Fallowfield CB4 ......19 A3	Cambridge CB1 ....35 B3	Great Shelford CB2 ...39 C1
Drayton Close CB1 ...35 C3	Fanshawe Road CB1 ..33 C4	Fulbourn CB1 ....29 C1	Granhams Close CB2 ..42 C4
Drayton Road CB1 ...35 C3	Farmer's Row CB1 ...37 A2	Fulbrooke Road CB3 ..24 C1	Granta Place CB2 ....45 A1
Drift The CB4 ....2 A3	Farmstead Close CB4 ..4 A3		Granta Terrace CB2 ..43 C2
Drosier Road CB1 ....45 C1	Farringford Close 4	**G**	**Grantchester Meadows**
Drummer Street CB1 .45 B2	CB4 ....17 B4		CB3 ....25 B1
Dudley Road CB5 ....20 A2	Faulkner Close CB4 ..12 B4	Gainsborough Close	**Grantchester Road**
Dukes Meadow CB2 ..43 B3	**Fawcett Primary Sch**	CB4 ....19 A4	Barton CB3 ....23 C1
Dundee Close CB4 ...18 C3	CB2 ....32 C1	Galfrid Road CB5 ....27 C4	Cambridge CB2 ....38 A4
Dunmowe Way CB1 ..37 A3	Fazeley CB1 ....45 C2	Garden Fields CB2 ....42 A1	Coton CB3 ....23 B3
Dunsmore Close CB5 .20 A2	Felton Street CB1 ....26 C2	**Garden Walk**	Grantchester CB2 .....32 A4
Durnford Way CB4 ...18 A3	Fen Causeway The CB3 45 A1	Cambridge CB4 ....17 C2	**Grantchester Street** 3
Dwyer-Joyce Close CB4 4 A2	**Fen Ditton Cp Sch** CB5 20 B3	Histon CB4 ....4 B3	CB3 ....25 B1
	Fen Road CB4 ....19 C4	Garlic Row CB5 ......19 A1	Grasmere Gardens CB1 44 A4
E	Fendon Close CB1 ....34 A1	Garner Close CB4 .....6 B1	Gray Road CB1 ......34 C4
	Fendon Road CB1 ....34 A1	Garret Hostel Lane CB2 45 A2	Grayling Close CB4 ...18 C2
Eachard Road CB3 ...17 A4	Fennec Close CB1 ....36 A4	Garry Drive CB4 .....11 C1	**Great & Little Shelford CE**
Earl Street CB1 ....45 B2	Fenners Lawn CB1 ...45 C1	Gayton Close 3 CB2 .32 C1	**Prim Sch** CB2 ....42 B2
East Hertford Street	Ferndale CB1 ....29 B2	Gazeley Road CB2 ....32 C2	Great Close CB3 ......30 A3
CB4 ....44 A4	Ferndale Rise CB5 ...19 B2	Gazelle Way CB1 .....29 A1	**Great Eastern Street**
East Road CB1 ......45 C2	Fernlea Close CB1 ....28 B1	Geoffrey Bishop Avenue	CB1 ....27 A2
Eastfield CB4 ....18 C3	Ferrars Way CB4 .....17 C4	CB1 ....37 C2	Greater Foxes CB1 ...37 B3
Eaton Close CB4 .....18 C4	Ferry Cutter Lane CB4 .44 C4	George IV Street CB2 .45 C1	Green End CB5 ......20 A4
Eden Street CB1 .....44 C3	Ferry Lane CB4 ......19 A2	**George Nuttall Close**	Green End Road CB5 .19 A4
Eden Street Backway	Ferry Path CB1 ......44 B4	CB4 ....18 C4	**Green Hedges Sch The**
CB1 ....45 C2	Field Lane CB5 ......20 A4	**George Pateman Court** 2	CB2 ....43 B2
Edendale Close CB1 ..34 B3	Field Way CB1 ....34 B1	CB1 ....26 B2	Green Park CB4 .....19 A4
Edgecombe CB4 .....11 B1	Finch Road CB4 .....17 C3	George Street CB4 ...18 B2	Green Street CB2 ....44 A3
Edinburgh Road CB4 .18 C3	Finch's Close CB2 ...43 B3	Gerard Close CB5 ....17 A4	Green The CB4 ......19 A3
Edmund Close CB4 ..12 B4	Fisher Street CB1 ....44 A4	Gerard Road CB1 ....19 C1	Greenfield Close CB2 .43 C2
Edward Street CB1 ..26 C2	Fisher's Lane CB1 ...35 B4	Gifford Place CB2 ....44 A3	Greenlands CB2 .....34 A1

50 Gre – Ley

Greenleas CB4 . . . . 4 A3
Green's Road CB4 . . . . . . 18 A2
Gresham Road CB1 . . . . 45 C1
Greville Road CB1 . . . . . 27 A1
Greystoke Court **1**
CB1 . . . . 35 A3
Greystoke Road CB1 . . . 35 A3
Grieve Court CB4 . . . . . . 19 B3
Grove Lane CB1 . . . . 45 B1
Grove Primary School The
CB4 . . . . 18 B4
Grove The CB4 . . . . 19 A4
Guest Road CB1 . . . . 45 C2
Guildhall Place **5** CB1 45 A2
Guildhall Street **3** CB1 45 A2
Gunhild Close CB1 . . . . 34 C3
Gunhild Court CB1 . . . . 34 B3
Gunhild Way CB1 . . . . . 34 B3
Gunnell Court CB4 . . . . 12 C4
Gunning Way CB4 . . . . . 17 B4
Gurney Way CB4 . . . . . . 18 A2
Gwydir Street CB1 . . . . . 26 C2

H

Hadleigh Court CB5 . . . . 20 A2
Haggis Gap CB1 . . . . 37 B3
Haig Court CB4 . . . . 18 C2
Hale Avenue CB4 . . . . . . 17 C2
Halifax Road CB4 . . . . . . 17 A2
Hall End CB4 . . . . 12 C4
Hall Farm Road **2** CB4 17 C3
Hamilton Road CB4 . . . . 44 B4
Hanover Court CB1 . . . . 45 B1
Hanson Court CB4 . . . . . 11 A1
Harcombe Road CB1 . . . 35 A4
Harding Way
 Cambridge CB4 . . . . 17 B3
 Histon CB4 . . . . 4 A2
Hardwick Street CB3 . . . 25 B1
Harebell Close CB1 . . . . 35 C3
Harris Road CB4 . . . . 17 C4
Harry Scott Court CB4 . . 11 A1
Hartington Grove CB1 . . 33 C3
Harvest Way CB1 . . . . . . 26 C2
Harvey Goodwin Avenue
CB4 . . . . 17 C2
Harvey Goodwin Gardens
CB4 . . . . 17 C2
Harvey Road CB1 . . . . . . 45 C1
Hatherdene Close CB1 . . 28 A2
Hauxton Road CB2 . . . . 38 B2
Haven The CB1 . . . . 37 B3
Haviland Way CB4 . . . . . 18 B2
Hawkins Road CB4 . . . . . 11 B1
Hawthorn Way CB4 . . . . 18 B2
Hawthorne Road CB2 . . 43 B2
Haymarket Road **7**
CB3 . . . . 17 B1
Hayster Drive CB1 . . . . . 35 A4
Hazelwood Close CB4 . . 17 C4
Headford Close CB5 . . . 19 C2
Headington Close CB1 . . 35 B3
Headington Drive CB1 . . 35 B3
Headley Gardens CB2 . . 43 A2
Heath House CB4 . . . . . . 18 C3
Hectare The CB2 . . . . 39 B1
Hedgerley Close CB3 . . . 24 C4
Heffer Close CB2 . . . . . . 43 B2
Helen Close **3** CB5 . . 20 A2
Hemingford Road CB1 . . 27 A2

Henley Road CB1 . . . . . . 27 A4
Henry Morris Road CB4 . 4 B1
Herbert Street CB4 . . . . 18 A2
Herbert Twinn Court
CB5 . . . . 19 C2
Hercules Close **5** CB4 . 11 A2
Hereward Close CB4 . . . . 4 B1
Heron's Close CB1 . . . . . 34 C2
Herring's Close CB5 . . . 22 B3
Herschel Road CB3 . . . 25 A3
Hertford Street CB4 . . . . 44 A4
Hicks Lane CB3 . . . . 9 A2
High Ditch Road CB5 . . 20 C2
High Green CB2 . . . . 42 C4
High Street Barton CB3 . 30 A2
 Cherry Hinton CB1 . . . . . . 28 C1
 Coton CB3 . . . . 23 A4
 Fen Ditton CB5 . . . . 20 A3
 Fulbourn CB1 . . . . 37 B3
 Girton CB3 . . . . 9 A3
 Grantchester CB3 . . . . 31 C2
 Great Shelford CB2 . . . . . 42 A1
 Histon CB4 . . . . 4 A2
 Horningsea CB5 . . . . 13 C3
 Landbeach CB4 . . . . 6 C4
 Madingley CB3 . . . . 14 B3
 Milton CB4 . . . . 12 C4
 Oakington CB4 . . . . 2 B4
 Stourbridge Common CB4 18 C2
 Teversham CB1 . . . . 29 B2
Highdene Road CB1 . . . 35 C4
Highfield Avenue CB4 . . 18 A3
Highfield Gate CB1 . . . . 37 B3
Highfield Road CB4 . . . . 10 B3
Highsett CB1 . . . . 45 C1
Highworth Avenue CB4 18 B3
Hilda Street CB4 . . . . 17 C2
Hills Avenue CB1 . . . . . . 34 A3
Hills Road CB2 . . . . 45 C1
Hills Road Sixth Form Coll
CB1 . . . . 33 C4
Hillstead CB2 . . . . 40 C1
Hinton Avenue CB1 . . . . 34 B3
Hinton Road CB1 . . . . . . 36 C3
Hinton Way CB2 . . . . 43 B4
**Histon & Impington Infant
School** CB4 . . . . 4 B2
Histon & Impington Jun Sch
CB4 . . . . 4 B2
Histon Road CB4 . . . . . . 17 B2
Histon Sch CB4 . . . . 4 A2
Hoadly Road CB3 . . . . . . 17 A3
Hobart Road CB1 . . . . . . 27 B1
Hobson Street CB1 . . . . 44 B3
Holben Close CB3 . . . . . 30 A1
Holbrook Road CB1 . . . . 34 A2
Hollmans Close CB1 . . . 37 B2
Hollymount **6** CB1 . . . 26 C2
Holme Close CB4 . . . . 2 B3
Holyrood Close CB4 . . . . 17 B4
Home Close CB4 . . . . 4 A2
Home End CB1 . . . . 37 C2
Homefield Close CB4 . . . 4 B1
Homerton Coll CB2 . . . 33 C3
Homerton Street CB2 . . 33 C4
Homing The CB5 . . . . . . 20 A1
Honey Hill **9** CB3 . . . . 17 B1
Honey Hill Mews CB3 . . 17 B1
Hooper Street CB1 . . . . . 26 C3
Hope Street CB1 . . . . 27 A2
Hopkins Close CB1 . . . . 18 C1
Horningsea Road
 Fen Ditton CB5 . . . . 20 B4

Horningsea Road continued
 Horningsea CB5 . . . . 13 C2
Howard Close CB5 . . . . 19 C2
Howard Court CB5 . . . . 20 A2
Howard Road CB5 . . . . . 20 A2
Howes Place CB3 . . . . . . 16 C3
Howgate Road CB4 . . . . 10 C1
Hulatt Road CB1 . . . . 34 B2
Humberstone Road
CB4 . . . . 44 C4
Humphreys Road CB4 . . 18 A4
Humphries Way CB4 . . . 6 C1
Huntingdon Road CB3 . 16 C3
Huntley Close CB5 . . . . . 20 A2
Huntsmill CB1 . . . . 37 A2
Hurrell Road CB4 . . . . . . 17 B4
Hurst Park Avenue CB4 18 A3

I

Ida Darwin Hospital
CB1 . . . . 36 C3
Impala Drive CB1 . . . . . . 28 C1
Impett's Lane CB1 . . . . . 37 C2
Impington Lane CB4 . . . . 4 B1
Impington Village Coll
CB4 . . . . 4 C1
Institute of Astronomy
CB3 . . . . 16 C1
Institute of Public Health
CB2 . . . . 40 A4
International Extension Coll
CB1 . . . . 26 C2
Inverness Close CB4 . . . 18 C3
Iver Close CB1 . . . . 28 B1
Ivy Field CB3 . . . . 30 A2
Izaak Walton Way CB4 . 19 B3

J

Jack Warren Green
CB5 . . . . 20 B1
James Nurse Close
CB1 . . . . 35 C4
James Street CB5 . . . . . . 44 B3
Jasmine Court CB1 . . . . 34 B3
Jedburgh Close **3** CB1 . 11 A1
Jermyn Close CB1 . . . . . 17 C4
Jesus Coll CB5 . . . . 44 B3
Jesus Lane CB1 . . . . 44 B3
Jesus Terrace CB1 . . . . . 44 C3
JJ Thompson Ave CB3 . 24 B4
John Clarke Court CB4 18 C1
John Conder Court
CB1 . . . . 27 B1
John Street CB1 . . . . 45 C2
Jolley Way CB4 . . . . 18 B4
Jordans Yard CB1 . . . . . . 44 A3
Joscelynes CB2 . . . . 43 B2
Junction The★ CB1 . . 33 C4

K

Kaldor Court **6** CB4 . . 11 A1
Kathleen Elliot Way
CB1 . . . . 28 B1
Kay Hitch Way CB4 . . . 10 A4
Keates Road CB1 . . . . . 35 C3
Kelsey Crescent CB1 . . . 28 C1
**Kelsey Kerridge Sports
Centre** CB1 . . . . 45 C1
Kelvin Close CB1 . . . . . . 34 C3
Kendal Way CB4 . . . . 18 C4

Kent Way CB4 . . . . 11 B1
Kerridge Close CB1 . . . 26 C3
Kettles Close CB4 . . . . . . 2 B3
Kettle's Yard★ CB1 . . . 44 A4
Keynes Road CB5 . . . . . 19 C2
**Kigezi International Sch of
Medicine** CB1 . . . . 45 B2
Kilmaine Close CB4 . . . 11 B2
Kimberley Road CB4 . . 44 C4
**King Hedges Primary
School** CB4 . . . . 11 B1
King Street CB1 . . . . 44 B3
King's Hedges Road
CB4 . . . . 10 C1
King's Lane CB1 . . . . 45 A2
King's Parade CB2 . . . . . 45 A2
King's Road CB1 . . . . 25 A1
Kings Coll CB2 . . . . 45 A2
Kings College School
CB3 . . . . 25 B1
Kings Grove CB3 . . . . . . 30 A2
Kings Mill Lane CB2 . . 42 B2
Kingston Street CB1 . . . 26 C2
Kingsway CB4 . . . . 17 C4
Kinnaird Way CB1 . . . . . 34 B2
Kinross Road CB4 . . . . . 18 C3
Kirby Close CB4 . . . . 18 B3
Kirkwood Road CB4 . . . 11 B1
Knights Way CB4 . . . . . . 6 C1

L

Laburnum Close CB4 . . 18 B2
Lady Adrian School The
CB4 . . . . 18 A3
Lady Jermy Way CB1 . . 29 A3
Lady Margaret Road 1
CB3 . . . . 17 B1
Lambourn Close **1**
CB2 . . . . 32 C1
Lammas Field **4** CB3 . 25 B1
Landbeach Road CB3 . . 6 C1
Lander Close CB4 . . . . . . 6 B1
Langdale Close CB1 . . 28 C1
Langham Road CB1 . . . 34 B4
Lansdowne Road CB3 . 16 B1
Lantree Crescent CB2 . 43 B2
Lapwings Close CB1 . . 29 A3
Larkin Close CB4 . . . . . . 18 C4
Larmor Drive CB3 . . . . . . 17 A1
Latham Close CB2 . . . . 32 C4
Latham Road CB2 . . . . . 32 C4
Latimer Close CB5 . . . . . 20 A1
Laundress Lane CB3 . . 45 A2
Laundry Lane CB1 . . . . 34 C3
Lauriston Place **1** CB4 11 A2
Lavender Road CB4 . . . 11 C1
Lawns The CB3 . . . . 24 C4
Lawrence Way CB4 . . . . 11 B1
Laxton Way CB4 . . . . 19 B4
Lees Way CB3 . . . . 9 A3
Leete Road CB1 . . . . 35 B3
Leeway Avenue CB2 . . . 43 B2
Legion Court CB4 . . . . . 11 A1
Lemur Drive CB1 . . . . . . 29 A1
Lensfield Road CB2 . . . 45 B1
Lents Way CB4 . . . . 19 B3
Leonard Close **2** CB5 . 20 A2
Lexington Close **3** CB4 17 B3
Leyburn Close CB1 . . . . 28 C1
Leys Avenue CB4 . . . . . 18 B3
Leys Road CB4 . . . . 18 B3
Leys Sch The CB2 . . . . 45 B1

Ley – Oys 51

Leys Sports Centre The
CB2 . . . . 26 A1
Lichfield Road CB1 . . . 34 A4
Lilac Court CB1 . . . . 34 B3
Lilley Close CB4 . . . . 19 A3
Limekiln Road CB1. . . . . 35 A1
Limetree Close **3** CB1 34 C3
Linden Close CB4 . . . . . . 17 B2
Lingholme Close **2**
CB4 . . . . 17 B3
Lingrey Court CB2 . . . . . 38 C2
Lion Yard Shopping Centre
CB1 . . . . 45 B2
Lisle Walk CB1 . . . . 35 C4
Little St Mary's Lane
CB2 . . . . 45 A1
Logan's Way CB4 . . . . . . 18 C1
London Road CB2 . . . . . 43 A2
Lone Tree Avenue CB4 . 10 B2
Lone Tree Grove CB4 . . . 10 B2
Long Road CB2 . . . . 33 B2
Long Road Sixth Form
College CB2 . . . . 33 B1
Long Reach Road CB4 . 19 B4
Longstanton Road CB4 . . 2 A1
Longworth Avenue CB4 18 C1
Loris Court CB1 . . . . 28 C1
Loughton Court CB5 . . . 20 A2
Lovell Road CB4 . . . . 11 C1
Love's Close CB4 . . . . . . 10 B4
Low Fen Drove Way
CB5 . . . . 21 A2
Lowbury Crescent CB4 . . 2 A4
Lower Park Street CB5 44 A3
Luard Close CB2 . . . . 33 C2
Luard Road CB2 . . . . 33 C3
Lucerne Close CB1 . . . . . 35 C4
Lucketts Close CB4 . . . . . 4 A3
Lucy Cavendish College
CB3 . . . . 17 B1
Ludlow Lane CB1 . . . . . . 37 C3
Lyndewode Road CB1 . 45 C1
Lyndhurst Close CB4 . . . 12 B4
Lynfield Lane CB4 . . . . . 18 C2
Lynx The CB1 . . . . 28 C1

M

MacAulay Avenue CB2 . 43 A4
Macfarlane Close CB4 . 10 B4
MacKenzie Road **5**
CB1 . . . . 26 C3
Madingley Hall★ CB3 . 14 A3
Madingley Road CB3 . . 17 A1
Madingley Sch CB3 . . . . 14 B3
Madingley Wood CB3 . 14 C2
Madras Road CB1 . . . . . . 27 B1
Magdalene Coll CB4 . . . 44 A4
Magdalene Street CB2 . 44 A3
Magnolia Close CB1 . . . 34 A3
Magrath Avenue CB4 . . 44 A4
Maid's Causeway CB5 . . 44 C3
Mailes Close CB3 . . . . . . 30 A2
Main Street CB5 . . . . 22 B3
Maio Road CB4 . . . . 18 B3
Maitland Avenue CB4 . . 19 A4
Malcolm Street CB1 . . . . 44 B3
Malden Close CB5 . . . . . 19 C1
Malletts Road CB1 . . . . . 35 C3
Malta Road CB1 . . . . 27 A1
Malting Lane CB3 . . . . . . 25 B2
Maltsters Way CB4 . . . . 18 C2
Malvern Road CB1 . . . . . 35 A4

Mander Way CB1 . . . . . . 34 B3
Mandrill Close CB1 . . . 28 C1
Maners Way CB1 . . . . . . 34 B2
Manhattan Drive CB4 . . 44 C4
Manor Community College
CB4 . . . . 18 B4
Manor Court CB3 . . . . . . 25 A2
Manor Farm Close CB4 . . 2 B4
Manor Farm Road CB3 . . 9 A4
Manor Park CB4 . . . . 3 C2
Manor Place CB1 . . . . . . 44 B3
Manor Road CB2 . . . . . . 42 A2
Manor Street CB1 . . . . . . 44 B3
Manor Walk CB1 . . . . . . 37 C3
Mansel Court CB4 . . . . . 18 A4
Mansel Way CB4 . . . . . . 18 A4
Mansfield Close CB4 . . 12 B4
Maple Close CB4 . . . . . . 18 B3
Maples The CB1 . . . . 37 A3
March Lane CB1 . . . . 28 B2
March's Close CB1 . . . . . 37 A3
Marfleet Close CB2 . . . . 39 B1
Mariner's Way CB4 . . . . 18 C1
Marion Close CB3 . . . . . 17 A2
Maris Green CB2 . . . . . . 42 C4
Maris Lane CB2 . . . . 38 B4
Market Hill CB2 . . . . 45 A2
Market Passage CB1 . . . 44 A3
Market Square CB2 . . . . 45 A2
Market Street CB1 . . . . . 44 A3
Markham Close CB4 . . . 11 C1
Mark's Way CB3 . . . . 9 A3
Marlborough Court
CB3 . . . . 25 A2
Marlowe Road CB3 . . . 25 B1
Marmora Road CB1 . . . 27 A1
Marshall Road CB1 . . . 33 C3
Marshall's Close CB1 . . 28 C3
Martingale Close **3**
CB4 . . . . 17 B4
Mawson Road CB1 . . . . . 45 C1
Mayfield Primary School
CB4 . . . . 17 B3
Mayfield Road CB3 . . . . . 9 B2
Mays Way CB4 . . . . 19 B3
Mead View CB4 . . . . 2 A3
Meadow Farm Close
CB4 . . . . 2 C4
Meadowlands Road
CB5 . . . . 20 A1
Melbourne Place CB1 . 45 C2
Melvin Way CB4 . . . . 3 C2
Mem Court CB3 . . . . 25 B3
Mercers Row CB5 . . . . . 19 A2
Mere Way CB4 . . . . 18 A4
Merton Road CB4 . . . . . . 4 A1
Merton Street CB3 . . . . . 25 B1
Metcalfe Road CB4 . . . . 17 C3
Michael's Close CB3 . . . . 9 A3
Midfield CB4 . . . . 2 C2
Midhurst Close CB4 . . . 18 C3
Milford Street CB1 . . . . 26 C3
Mill Court CB2 . . . . 42 C2
Mill End Close CB1 . . . 35 B3
Mill End Road CB1 . . . . 35 A4
Mill Lane Cambridge CB2 45 A2
 Histon CB4 . . . . 4 C4
 Impington CB4 . . . . 4 C3
Mill Street CB1 . . . . 45 C1

Mill Way CB3 . . . . 31 C1
Millington Road CB3 . . 25 B1
Milton CE Primary Sch
CB4 . . . . 12 B4
Milton Country Park★
CB4 . . . . 12 C3
Milton Road
 Cambridge CB4 . . . . 44 B4
 Impington CB4 . . . . 5 B2
Milton Road Primary
School CB4 . . . . 18 A2
Minerva Way CB4 . . . . . 11 A2
Mingle Lane CB2 . . . . . . 43 A3
Minter Close CB5 . . . . . . 22 C3
Missleton Court CB1 . . 34 B3
Misty Meadows CB5 . . . 19 C2
Molewood Close CB4 . . 17 B4
Moncrieff Close **1** CB4 11 A1
Monkswell CB2 . . . . 32 C1
Montfort Way CB4 . . . . 18 A4
Montgomery Road CB4 18 A4
Montreal Road CB1 . . . 27 B1
Montrose Close CB4 . . . 11 A1
Moore Close CB4 . . . . . . 18 C4
More's Meadow CB2 . . 42 B4
Morley Memorial Prim Sch
CB1 . . . . 34 A3
Mortimer Road CB1 . . . 45 C2
Mortlock Avenue CB4 . . 19 A4
Moss Bank CB4 . . . . 19 B3
Mount Pleasant **3** CB3 17 B1
Mount Pleasant Walk **2**
CB3 . . . . 17 B1
Mowbray Road CB1 . . . 34 B2
Mowlam Close CB4 . . . 10 B4
Moyne Close CB4 . . . . . 10 C1
Mulberry Close CB4 . . . 18 B3
Mumford Theatre★
CB1 . . . . 45 C2
Muncey Walk CB4 . . . . . . 4 B3
Museum of Archaeology
and Anthropology★
CB2 . . . . 45 B2
Museum of Classical
Archaeology★ CB3 . . 25 B2
Museum of Technology★
CB5 . . . . 19 A1
Musgrave Way CB5 . . . 20 B4

N

Napier Street CB1 . . . . . 44 C3
Narrow Lane CB4 . . . . . . 4 A2
Natal Road CB1 . . . . 27 B1
National Extension Coll
CB2 . . . . 26 B1
Neale Close CB1 . . . . 28 B1
Neptune Close CB4 . . . . 11 A1
Netherhall Sch The
CB1 . . . . 35 A2
Netherhall Way CB1 . . . 34 C2
Neville Road CB1 . . . . . 34 B4
New Hall CB3 . . . . 17 B1
New Park Street CB5 . . 44 A4
New Road Barton CB3 . . 30 A2
 Histon CB4 . . . . 4 B1
New School Road CB4 . . 4 A1
New Square CB1 . . . . . . 44 B3
New Street CB1 . . . . 26 C4
Newell Walk CB1 . . . . . . 28 B1
Newmarket Road
 Cambridge CB5 . . . . 44 C3
 Fen Ditton CB1 . . . . 21 C1

Newmarket Road continued
 Stow cum Quy CB5 . . . . . 22 B2
Newnham Coll CB3 . . 25 B2
Newnham Croft Prim Sch
CB3 . . . . 25 B1
Newnham Croft Street **2**
CB3 . . . . 25 B1
Newnham Road CB3 . . . 25 B1
Newnham Terrace CB1 45 A1
Newnham Terr CB3 . . . 25 B2
Newnham Walk CB3 . . . 25 B2
Newton Road CB2 . . . . . 33 A3
Nicholson Way CB4 . . . 18 A4
Nightingale Avenue
CB1 . . . . 34 B1
Norfolk Street CB1 . . . . . 26 C3
Norfolk Terrace CB1 . . . 26 C3
Normanton Way CB4 . . 4 A3
North Cottages CB2 . . . 32 C2
North Street CB4 . . . . . . 17 B2
North Terrace CB1 . . . . . 44 C3
Northampton Street
CB3 . . . . 25 B4
Northfield Fulbourn CB1 37 C3
 Girton CB3 . . . . 9 A4
Northfields Avenue
CB4 . . . . 11 A1
Northumberland Close **2**
CB4 . . . . 17 C4
Norton Close CB5 . . . . . 19 C1
Norwich Street CB2 . . . . 26 A1
Nuffield Close CB4 . . . . 12 A1
Nuffield Road CB4 . . . . . 19 A4
Nun's Orchard CB4 . . . . 4 A2
Nuns Way CB4 . . . . 11 B1
Nursery Walk CB4 . . . . . 17 B3
Nutters Close CB3 . . . . . 31 C2
Nuttings Road CB1 . . . . 27 C3

O

Oak Tree Avenue CB4 . . 18 B3
Oak Tree Way CB4 . . . . . . 4 A1
Oakington CE Prim Sch
CB4 . . . . 2 B3
Oakington Road CB3 . . . 3 A1
Oaks The CB4 . . . . 12 B4
Occupation Road CB1 . 26 C4
Old Farm Close CB4 . . . . 4 A3
Old School Lane CB4 . . 12 C4
Ongar Court CB5 . . . . . . 20 B2
Open Univ The CB2 . . . 45 C1
Orchard Avenue CB4 . . . 18 A3
Orchard Close CB3 . . . . . 9 A3
Orchard Drive CB4 . . . . . 9 A1
Orchard Estate CB1 . . . 28 B1
Orchard Road
 Great Shelford CB2 . . . . . 43 A4
 Histon CB4 . . . . 4 B3
Orchard Street
 Cambridge CB1 . . . . 44 B3
 Stow cum Quy CB5 . . . . . 22 B3
Orchard Way CB4 . . . . . . 2 B3
Orchards The
 Cambridge CB1 . . . . 35 B3
 Great Shelford CB2 . . . . . 43 A4
Orwell Furlong CB4 . . . 12 B1
Oslar's Way CB1 . . . . 37 A3
Owlstone Road CB3 . . 25 B1
Oxford Road CB4 . . . . . . 17 A2
Oyster Row CB5 . . . . 19 A1

52 Pad – St N

P

Paddock Close CB4 ..... 4 B2
Paddocks The CB1 .....27 B3
Paget Close CB2 ....33 A1
Paget Road CB2 ....38 C2
Pakenham Close CB4 ...18 C3
Palmers Walk CB1 .....14 C2
Pamplin Court **1** CB1 ..35 B4
Panther Way CB1 .....28 C1
Panton Street CB2 .....45 B1
Paradise Nature Reserve★
CB1 ....45 A1
Paradise Street CB1 ...44 C3
Park Avenue CB4 ....3 C2
Park Drive CB4 .... 4 B1
Park Lane Histon CB4 ....3 B2
Madingley CB3 ....14 B4
Park Parade CB5 ......44 A4
Park Street CB1 ......44 B3
Park Street CE Prim Sch
CB5 ....44 B3
Park Terrace CB1 ......45 B2
Parker Street CB1 .....45 B2
Parker's Terrace **2**
CB1 ....26 C4
Parkside CB1 ....45 C2
Parkside Foundation Coll
CB1 ....45 C2
Parkside Pools CB1 ....45 C2
Parlour Close CB4 ...... 4 A3
Parr Close CB4 .... 4 B1
Parsonage Street CB5 ..44 C3
Parson's Court CB2 ....45 A2
Pavilion Court **7** CB4 ..11 A2
Peacocks CB2 ....42 C2
Pearce Close CB3 .....25 A2
Pearmain Court CB4 ...19 B3
Pearson Close CB4 ....12 C3
Peas Hill CB2 ....45 A2
Pease Way CB4 .... 3 B2
Pelham Court CB4 .....17 B4
Pelican Prep Sch CB1 ..34 C2
Pemberton Terrace
CB2 ....45 B1
Pembroke Coll CB2 ...45 A2
Pembroke Street CB2 ..45 A2
Pembroke Way CB1 ...29 A3
Pen Close CB1 ....35 C4
Penarth Place CB3 ....24 C2
Pentlands Close CB4 ..44 C4
Pentlands Court CB1 ..44 C4
Pepys Terrace CB4 ....10 B3
Pepys Way CB3 .... 9 A2
Percheron Close CB4 ... 4 C1
Perne Avenue CB1 ....34 B4
Perne Road CB1 ......34 B4
Perowne Street CB1 ..26 C3
Perry Court CB3 ......24 C1
Perse Boys Sch The
CB2 ....33 C2
Perse Girls 6Th Form
College CB1 ....45 C1
Perse Prep Sch CB2 ...33 A2
Perse Sch For Girls The
CB2 ....45 B1
Perse Way CB4 ....17 C3
Peter Goodin Close
CB4 ....12 B4
Peterhouse CB2 ....45 A1

Peterhouse Technology
Park CB1 ....35 C2
Petersfield **3** CB1 ......45 C2
Pettits Close CB1 .....37 B2
Petty Cury CB2 ....45 A2
Petworth Street CB1 ...26 C4
Peverel Close CB5 .....19 C1
Peverel Road CB5 .....19 C1
Pierce Lane CB1 ......37 B3
Pikes Walk CB1 ....44 B3
Pippin Drive CB4 .....19 B4
Plum Tree Close **3**
CB4 ....10 C1
Poplar Close CB2 .....42 C3
Poplar Road CB4 ...... 4 A1
Poplar Way CB2 ......43 B2
Porson Court CB2 ....33 A2
Porson Road CB2 ....32 C3
Portland Place CB1 ...44 C3
Portugal Place CB2 ...44 A3
Portugal Street CB5 ..44 A3
Post Office Terrace
CB1 ....45 B2
Pound Hill CB3 ....17 B1
Pretoria Road CB4 ....44 C4
Priam's Way CB2 .....43 A2
Primary Court CB4 ...19 A3
Primrose Close CB1 ...35 C3
Primrose Street CB4 ..17 C2
Prince William Court **6**
CB4 ....17 B2
Princess Court CB1 ...45 B1
Prior's Close CB4 ..... 4 A2
Priory Road
Cambridge CB5 ....18 C1
Horningsea CB5 ....13 C3
Priory Street **3** CB4 ...17 B2
Prospect Row CB1 ...45 C2
Pryor Close CB4 ......12 C2
Purbeck Road CB2 ...33 C3
Pye Terrace CB4 ......18 C2

Q

Quainton Close CB5 ....19 C1
Quayside CB1 ....44 A3
Queen Edith Community
Prim Sch CB1 ....34 B2
Queen Edith's Way CB1 34 C2
Queen's Marlborough Coll
The CB2 ....26 A1
Queen's Meadow CB1 ..28 B1
Queen's Road CB3 ....25 B2
Queens Coll CB3 ......45 A2
Queens' Lane CB2 ....45 A2
Queens Way CB4 ...... 2 C4
Queensway CB2 ......33 A4

R

Rachel Close **1** CB5 ....20 A2
Rackham Close CB4 ...17 B2
Radegund Road CB1 ..27 A1
Railway Street CB1 ...28 B1
Ramsden Square CB4 ..11 C1
Rathmore Close CB1 ..33 C4
Rathmore Road CB1 ..33 C4
Ravensworth Gardens
CB1 ....26 C1
Rawlyn Close CB5 ....19 C1
Rawlyn Court CB5 ....19 C1
Rawlyn Road CB5 ....19 C1
Rayleigh Close CB2 ...33 A3

Rayson Way CB5 ....19 C1
Recreation Close CB4 ..12 C3
Red Cross Lane CB2 ..34 A1
Red Hill Close CB2 ....39 A2
Red Hill Lane CB2 ....39 A2
Redfern Close CB4 ....18 A4
Redgate Road CB3 ..... 9 A2
Regatta Court CB5 ...19 A2
Regency Square CB1 ..26 C1
Regent Street CB2 ....45 B1
Regent Terrace CB2 ...45 B1
Reilly Way CB1 ....28 B2
Ribston Way CB4 .....19 B4
Richmond Road CB4 ..17 A2
Richmond Terrace CB1 44 A4
Rickard Close CB1 ....35 A4
Ridgefield Primary School
CB1 ....27 B1
Ridley Hall Road CB3 ..25 B2
Rivar Place CB1 ......26 C3
River Lane CB5 ....18 C1
Riverside CB5 ....19 A1
Riverside Court CB1 ..44 B4
Robert Jennings Close
CB4 ....18 C4
Robert May Close CB1 .27 C1
Robinson College CB3 .25 A3
Robinson Way CB2 ...33 C1
Rock Road CB1 ......33 C4
Rodings The CB5 .....20 A2
Roedeer Close CB1 ...28 C1
Roland Close CB4 ....18 A3
Roman Courts CB4 ...11 A2
Roman Hill CB3 ......30 B2
Romsey Jun Sch CB1 .27 A2
Romsey Mews CB1 ...27 A1
Romsey Road CB1 ...27 B2
Romsey Terrace CB1 ..27 A1
Rose Crescent CB2 ...44 A3
Roseford Road CB4 ..17 C4
Roselea CB4 .... 4 B1
Rosemary Lane CB1 ..28 A1
Rosie Hospital CB2 ...33 C1
Ross Street CB1 ......27 A2
Rotherwick Way CB1 ..34 B1
Rothleigh Road **2** CB1 34 C3
Round Church Street
CB2 ....44 A3
Rowans The CB4 .....12 B3
Rowlinson Way CB4 ..19 A1
Roxburgh Road CB4 ..11 A1
Rupert Brooke Museum★
CB2 ....31 C1
Rush Grove CB1 ......35 C4
Russell Court CB2 ....26 A1
Russell Street CB1 ...45 C1
Russet Court CB4 ....19 B4
Rustat Avenue CB1 ...26 C1
Rustat Road CB1 .....33 C4
Rutherford Road CB2 .33 A2
Rutland Close CB4 ...17 C4

S

Sable Close CB1 ......28 C1
Sackville Close CB4 ..11 A1
Sadlers Close CB3 ....23 A4
Saffron Road CB4 ..... 4 A1
St Alban's Rc Primary Sch
CB2 ....45 B1

St Albans Road CB4 ...17 C4
St Andrew's CE Community
Jun Sch CB4 ....19 B4
St Andrew's Close CB2 43 B2
St Andrew's Park CB4 .. 4 A3
St Andrew's Road CB .18 C1
St Andrew's Street CB2 45 B2
St Andrews Way CB4 ... 5 A2
St. Anthonys Walk CB2 26 A1
St Audrey's Close CB4 . 3 C2
St Barnabas Road CB1 .26 C2
St Bartholomew's Court
CB5 ....19 A1
St Bede's Crescent CB1 35 A4
St Bede's Gardens CB1 35 A4
St Bede's Inter Church
Comp Sch CB1 ....34 C4
St Catharine's Coll CB2 45 A2
St Catharines Hall CB3 23 B4
St Catharines Square
CB4 ....10 B1
St Catherines Prep Sch
CB2 ....26 A1
St Christophers Avenue **2**
CB4 ....17 B2
St. Clements Gardens
CB1 ....44 A3
St Colettes Prep Sch
CB1 ....26 C1
St. Edmunds College
CB3 ....17 B1
St Edwards Passage **4**
CB1 ....45 A2
St Faiths Sch CB2 .....33 A4
St Georges Way CB4 ... 5 A2
St John's Coll CB2 ....44 A3
St John's Lane CB5 ...13 C4
St John's Place CB4 ..17 B1
St John's Road
Cambridge CB5 ....44 A4
Coton CB3 ....23 A4
St John's Street CB2 ..44 A3
St. Johns College School
CB3 ....25 B4
St John's Innovation Centre
CB4 ....12 B2
St Kilda Avenue CB4 ..11 C1
St. Laurence's Rc Primary
School CB4 ....10 C1
St. Luke's CE Primary
School CB4 ....17 B2
St. Lukes Mews CB4 ..17 C2
St Lukes Street CB4 ..44 A4
St Margaret's Road
CB3 ....16 B4
St Margaret's Square
CB1 ....34 A3
St Marks Court CB3 ..25 B2
St Mary's Passage **2**
CB1 ....45 A2
St Mary's Street **1** CB1 45 A2
St. Marys Passage CB1 45 A2
St Marys Sch CB2 ....26 A1
St Matthew's Court **5**
CB1 ....26 C4
St Matthew's Gardens
CB1 ....26 C4
St Matthew's Prim Sch
CB1 ....45 C2
St. Matthew's Street
CB1 ....26 C4
St Neots Road
Coton CB3 ....15 A1

St Neots Road continued
  Madingley CB3 . . . .**14** B1
St Paul's CE Primary Sch
  CB2 . . . .**45** B1
St Paul's Road CB1 . . . . . .**45** C1
St. Pauls Walk CB1 . . . . . .**45** C1
St Peter's Road CB3 . . .**23** A4
St Peter's Street CB3 . . .**17** B1
St. Peters Terrace CB1 .**45** B1
St Philip's CE Prim Sch
  CB1 . . . .**45** B1
St Philip's Road CB1 . . .**27** A2
St Philips Road CB1 . . . .**27** B2
St. Regis CB4 . . . .**18** B2
St Stephen's Place ◼1
CB4 . . . .**17** B2
St Thomas's Square
  CB1 . . . .**34** C4
St Tibb's Row CB2 . . . . .**45** B2
St Vigor's Road CB1 . . . .**37** B2
St Vincent's Close CB3 . .**9** A2
Salisbury Villas CB1 . . . .**26** B1
Salmon Lane CB1 . . . .**44** C3
Sancton Wood Sch
  CB1 . . . .**45** C1
Sandwich Close ◼2 CB4 **11** A2
Sandy Lane CB4 . . . .**18** B2
Saxon Road CB5 . . . .**18** C1
Saxon Street CB2 . . . . . .**45** B1
Scarsdale Close CB4 . . .**19** A4
Sch of Clinical Medicine
  CB2 . . . .**34** C2
Schlumberger Laboratories
  CB3 . . . .**16** A1
School Hill CB4 . . . .**4** A2
School Lane Barton CB3 **30** A2
  Fulbourn CB1 . . . .**37** B2
  Histon CB4 . . . .**4** B1
Scotland Close CB4 . . . .**19** A3
Scotland Road CB4 . . . .**18** C3
Scotsdowne Road CB2 **32** C1
Scott Polar Research
  Institute CB2 . . . .**45** B1
Searle Street CB4 . . . . . .**17** C2
Sedgwick Museum of Earth
  Sciences★ CB2 . . . .**45** B2
Sedgwick Street CB1 . .**27** A2
Sedley Inf Sch CB1 . . . .**27** B1
Sedley Taylor Road
  CB2 . . . .**33** B2
Sefton Close CB2 . . . . . .**32** C1
Selwyn Close CB2 . . . . .**42** C3
Selwyn Coll CB3 . . . . . .**25** A2
Selwyn Gardens CB3 . .**25** A2
Selwyn Road CB3 . . . . .**25** A1
Senate House Passage
  CB2 . . . .**45** A2
Severn Place CB1 . . . . .**26** C4
Seymour Court CB1 . . .**27** B2
Seymour Street CB1 . . .**27** B2
Shaftesbury Road CB2 .**33** B4
Shelford Mill CB2 . . . . . .**42** B2
Shelford Park Avenue
  CB2 . . . .**42** C3
Shelford Road
  Cambridge CB2 . . . .**39** A2
  Fulbourn CB1 . . . .**36** B1
Shelford Sta CB2 . . . . . .**43** A3
Shelly Garden CB3 . . . .**17** B1
Shelly Row ◼4 CB3 . . . .**17** B1
Shepherd's Close
  Cambridge CB1 . . . .**35** C4
  Fen Ditton CB5 . . . .**20** B3

Sheppard Way CB1 . . . .**29** A3
Sherbourne Close CB4 **19** A4
Sherlock Close CB3 . . .**17** A2
Sherlock Court CB3 . . .**17** A2
Sherlock Road CB3 . . . .**17** A3
Shirley Close CB4 . . . . .**13** A4
Shirley Grove CB4 . . . . .**19** A3
Shirley Infant Sch CB4 .**19** A3
Shirley Road CB4 . . . .**4** A1
Short Street CB1 . . . . . .**44** B3
Sidgwick Avenue CB3 . .**25** B2
Sidney Farm Road CB1 **35** A4
Sidney Street CB2 . . . .**44** A3
Sidney Sussex Coll CB1 **44** B3
Silver Street CB3 . . . . . .**45** A1
Silverdale Avenue CB3 .**23** A4
Silverwood Close CB1 .**27** A4
Sleaford Street CB1 . . .**26** C3
Somerset Close CB4 . .**10** C1
Somerset Road CB4 . . . .**3** C1
Somervell Court ◼5
  CB2 . . . .**11** A1
South Green Road CB3 **25** B1
South Road CB4 . . . .**10** A3
Southacre Close CB2 . .**33** A4
Southacre Drive CB2 . .**33** A4
Southbrooke Close ◼2
  CB2 . . . .**32** C1
Southcourts CB1 . . . . . .**42** B1
Southside Court CB4 . .**18** C3
Spalding Way CB1 . . . . .**34** C2
Speedwell Close CB1 . .**35** C4
Spens Avenue CB3 . . . .**25** A2
Spinney Drive CB2 . . . .**42** C2
Spinney Prim Sch The
  CB1 . . . .**35** A4
Spring Close CB4 . . . .**4** B2
Springfield Road CB4 . .**18** A2
Springfield Terrace ◼1
  CB4 . . . .**18** A2
Spurgeon's Close CB1 .**29** A3
Square The CB5 . . . .**22** C4
Staffordshire Gardens ◼8
  CB1 . . . .**26** C3
Staffordshire Street
  CB1 . . . .**26** C4
Stanbury Close CB5 . . .**20** A4
Stanesfield Road CB5 .**19** C1
Stanley Court CB5 . . . .**19** A1
Stanley Road CB5 . . . . .**19** A1
Stansfield Gardens CB1 **37** B3
Stansgate Avenue CB2 .**34** A1
Stapleford Com Prim Sch
  CB2 . . . .**43** B2
Starling Close CB4 . . . . . .**6** C1
Station Road
  Cambridge CB1 . . . .**26** B1
  Fulbourn CB1 . . . .**37** C3
  Great Shelford CB2 . . . . . .**42** C3
  Histon CB4 . . . .**4** B1
Sterndale Close CB3 . . . .**9** A2
Sterne Close CB1 . . . . .**34** A4
Sternes Way CB2 . . . . .**43** B2
Stevenson Court CB5 . .**18** C1
Stirling Close CB4 . . . . .**18** C3
Stockwell Street CB1 . .**27** A2
Stone Street CB1 . . . . .**27** A3
Stone Terrace CB1 . . . .**27** A3
Stonebridge Lane CB1 .**37** C2
Stonehill Road CB2 . . . .**39** A1
Storey's Way CB3 . . . . .**17** A1
Stott Gardens CB4 . . . .**18** C4
Stourbridge Grove CB1 **27** B3

Stow Road CB5 . . . .**22** B3
Strangeways Road CB1 **34** C2
Stratfield Close CB4 . . .**17** A3
Strathcarron Court
  CB4 . . . .**11** A1
Stretten Avenue CB4 . .**17** C2
Stukeley Close CB3 . . .**24** C2
Stulp Field Road CB3 . .**31** C2
Sturmer Close ◼6 CB4 .**10** B1
Sturton Street CB1 . . . .**26** C3
Suez Road CB1 . . . .**27** B1
Summerfield CB3 . . . . . .**25** B2
Sun Street ◼1 CB1 . . . .**26** C4
Sunflower Street CB4 .**10** C1
Sunmead Walk CB1 . . .**35** C4
Sunnyside CB5 . . . .**28** A4
Sunset Square ◼2 CB4 **10** C1
Sussex Street CB2 . . . .**44** B3
Sutton Close CB4 . . . .**6** C1
Swann Road CB5 . . . . . .**19** B2
Swann's Road CB5 . . . .**19** A2
Swann's Terrace ◼4
  CB1 . . . .**26** C2
Swifts Corner CB1 . . . . .**37** B3
Sycamore Close ◼4
  CB1 . . . .**26** C3
Sycamores The CB4 . . .**12** B4
Sylvester Road CB3 . . .**25** A3
Symonds Close CB4 . . . .**4** A2

T
Tabrum Close CB3 . . . . .**31** B2
Tamarin Gardens CB1 .**35** C4
Taunton Close CB1 . . . .**27** C1
Tavistock Road CB4 . . .**17** B4
Teasel Way CB1 . . . .**35** C3
Tedder Way CB1 . . . .**17** B4
Temple Court ◼4 CB4 .**11** A1
Templemore Close CB1 **34** C2
Tenby Close CB1 . . . . . .**35** C4
Tenison Avenue CB1 . .**26** B1
Tenison Road CB1 . . . . .**26** C2
Tennis Court Road CB2 **45** B1
Tennis Court Terrace
  CB2 . . . .**45** A1
Teversham CE Prim Sch
  CB1 . . . .**29** A4
Teversham Drift CB1 . .**28** C1
Teversham Road CB1 . .**37** A4
Teynham Close CB1 . . .**27** C1
Thetford Terrace CB5 . .**28** A4
Thirleby Close CB4 . . . .**17** C3
Thoday Street CB1 . . . .**27** A2
Thomas Road CB1 . . . . .**36** C3
Thompson's Lane CB4 .**44** A3
Thorleye Road CB5 . . . .**27** B4
Thornton Close CB3 . . .**16** A4
Thornton Road CB3 . . . . .**9** B1
Thornton Way CB3 . . . .**16** A4
Thorpe Way CB5 . . . .**20** B2
Thrifts Walk CB4 . . . . . .**18** C2
Thulborn Close CB1 . . .**29** A3
Tillyard Way CB1 . . . . . .**34** C2
Tiptree Close CB5 . . . . .**20** B2
Tiverton Way CB1 . . . . .**27** B1
Topcliffe Way CB1 . . . .**34** B1
Topham Way CB4 . . . . .**17** C4
Townsend Close CB4 . . .**6** C1
Trafalgar Road CB4 . . .**44** B4
Trafalgar Street CB4 . .**44** B4
Tredegar Close CB4 . . .**18** A4
Tredgold Lane CB1 . . . .**44** C3

St N – Wal   53

Trevone Place CB1 . . . .**27** C1
Tribune Court CB4 . . . .**11** A1
Trinity Coll CB2 . . . .**44** B3
Trinity Lane CB2 . . . . . .**45** A2
Trinity Street CB2 . . . . .**45** A2
Trumpington Gallery★
  CB2 . . . .**18** A2
Trumpington High Street
  CB2 . . . .**32** C1
Trumpington Road CB2 **33** A3
Trumpington Street
  CB2 . . . .**45** A2
Tunwells Close CB2 . . .**42** C3
Tunwells Lane CB2 . . . .**42** C3
Turpyn Court CB4 . . . . .**18** A2
Tweedale CB2 . . . .**35** B3

U
Ucles CB1 . . . .**45** C1
Union Lane CB4 . . . .**18** B3
Union Road CB2 . . . .**45** B1
Univ Arts Sch CB2 . . . .**45** A2
University Museum of
  Zoology★ CB2 . . . .**45** B2
Univ of Cambridge
  Cambridge CB1 . . . .**26** C4
  Madingley CB3 . . . .**14** B1
University Concert Hall
  CB3 . . . .**25** B2
University Music School
  CB3 . . . .**25** B2
Uphall Road CB1 . . . . . .**27** C1
Upper Gwydir Street ◼1
  CB1 . . . .**26** C3

V
Valerian Court CB1 . . . .**35** C3
Valparaiso University
  CB3 . . . .**17** B1
Velos Walk CB5 . . . .**20** A2
Ventress Close CB1 . . .**34** C3
Ventress Farm Court
  CB1 . . . .**35** A3
Verulam Way CB4 . . . . .**17** C4
Vicarage Close CB4 . . . .**2** C4
Vicarage Drive CB3 . . . .**31** C1
Vicarage Terrace CB1 . .**26** C3
Victoria Avenue CB5 . .**44** B3
Victoria Park CB4 . . . . .**17** C2
Victoria Road CB4 . . . . .**17** C2
Victoria Street CB1 . . . .**45** B2
Villa Court CB4 . . . .**11** A2
Villa Place CB4 . . . .**10** B4
Villa Road CB4 . . . .**10** B4
Vine Close CB2 . . . .**43** B2
Vinery Park CB1 . . . .**27** B2
Vinery Road CB1 . . . . . .**27** B2
Vinery Way CB1 . . . .**27** B3
Violet Close CB1 . . . . . .**35** C3

W
Wadloes Road CB5 . . . .**19** C2
Wagstaff Close CB4 . . .**11** B1
Walden Way CB2 . . . . . .**42** B4
Walker Court CB1 . . . . .**18** A4
Walkling Way CB4 . . . . .**12** C3
Walnut Tree Avenue
  CB5 . . . .**18** C1

Wal – Zet

Walnut Tree Way CB4 ..10 B1
Walpole Road CB1 ....34 C4
Ward Road CB1 ....34 C4
Warkworth Street CB1 .45 C2
Warkworth Terrace
CB1..................45 C2
Warren Road CB4 ......18 C4
Warwick Road CB4 ....17 B3
Washpit Road CB3 .....8 C2
Water Lane
Cambridge CB4 ....19 A3
Histon CB4 .... 4 B1
Oakington/Longstanton CB4 2 B3
Water Street CB4 ......19 A2
Wavell Way CB4 ....18 A4
Weavers Field CB3 ......9 A1
Wedgewood Drive CB1 35 B4
Wellbrook Way CB3 .....9 B1
Wellington Court 3
CB1..................26 C4
Wellington Street 4
CB1..................26 C4
Welstead Road CB1 ....35 C4
Wentworth Road CB4 ..17 B2
Wenvoe Close CB1 .....35 B4
Wesley House CB5 .....44 B3
West Road
Cambridge CB3 ....25 B3
Histon CB4 .... 4 A1

West View CB3 ....25 B1
Westberry Court CB3 ..25 A2
Westcott House Theological
College CB1 ....44 B3
Westering The CB5 .....28 A4
Westfield Lane CB4 ....17 B2
Westfield Road CB2 ...39 A1
Westgate CB1 ....35 A3
Westminster & Cheshunt
Colleges CB3 ....17 B1
Weston Grove CB1 .....37 A3
Wetenhall Road CB1 ...27 A2
Wheeler Street CB2 ...45 A2
Wheelers CB2 ....43 A4
Wheelwright Way CB5 .22 C3
Whipple Museum of The
History of Science★
CB1....................45 A2
White Rose Walk 5
CB4....................10 C1
Whitefriars CB4 ....19 A3
Whitegate Close CB3 ...9 A2
Whitehill Close CB1 ....27 C4
Whitehill Road CB5 ....27 B4
Whitehouse Lane CB3 ..16 C1
Whitfield Close CB4 ....11 A1
Whitgift Road CB1 .....29 A3
Whitlocks CB2 ....38 C4
Whytford Close CB4 ...18 C1
Wilberforce Road CB3 .25 A4
Wilderspin Close CB3 ..16 B4

Wilding Walk CB4 ......18 C3
Wiles Close CB4 ....11 C1
Wilkin Street 1 CB1 ...26 C2
William Smith Close
CB1....................26 C1
Willis Road CB1 ....45 C2
Willow Crescent CB4 ..12 C4
Willow Walk CB1 ......44 B3
Wilson Close CB4 .....11 C1
Wilson Way CB4 ......12 C4
Winchmore Drive CB2 .32 B1
Winderemere Close
CB1..................28 C1
Winders Lane CB4 ......4 A3
Windlesham Close
CB4..................18 A4
Windmill Lane
Fulbourn CB1 ....37 A2
Histon CB4 .... 4 A2
Windmill Sch The CB1 .36 C3
Windsor Road CB4 ....17 B3
Wingate Close CB2 ....32 C1
Wingate Way CB2 ....32 C1
Winship Road CB4 ....12 B3
Woburn Close CB4 ....11 A1
Wolfson Coll CB3 .....25 A2
Wollaston Road CB1 ...45 C1
Wolsey Way CB1 ......28 B1
Woodcock Close CB4 ...4 C1
Woodhead Drive CB4 ..18 B4
Woodhouse Way CB4 ..11 C1

Woodlands Close
Girton CB3 .... 8 C3
Great Shelford CB2 .....42 C1
Woodlands Park CB3 ....8 C3
Woodlands Road CB2 ..42 C2
Woodlark Road CB3 ...17 A3
Woodmans Way CB4 ..12 C4
Woollards Lane CB2 ...42 C2
Wootton Way CB3 .....24 C2
Wordsworth Grove CB3 25 B2
Worts' Causeway CB1 ..40 B4
Wright's Close CB5 ....20 A4
Wrights Grove CB1 ....37 B2
Wulfstan Court CB1 ...34 B2
Wulfstan Way CB1 ....34 B2
Wycliffe Road CB1 .....27 B2
Wynborne Close CB4 ..18 A3
Wynford Way CB4 .....11 B1

Y

Yarrow Road CB1 .....35 C3
York Street CB1 ....26 C3
York Terrace CB1 ......26 C3
Young Street CB1 .....26 C4
Youngman Avenue CB4 .4 B3
Youngman Close CB4 ..4 B3
Zetland Walk CB1 ......27 C1

List of numbered locations

In some busy areas of the maps it is not always possible to show the name of every place.

Where not all names will fit, some smaller places are shown by a number. If you wish to find out the name associated with a number, use this listing.

The places in this list are also listed normally in the Index.

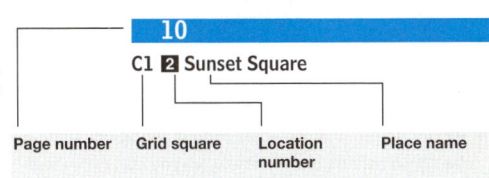

Example: **10** C1 **2** Sunset Square — Page number, Grid square, Location number, Place name

10
- B1 **6** Sturmer Close
- C1 **1** Crispin Close
- **2** Sunset Square
- **3** Plum Tree Close
- **4** Aylesborough Close
- **5** White Rose Walk

11
- A1 **1** Moncrieff Close
- **2** Banff Close
- **3** Jedburgh Close
- **4** Temple Court
- **5** Somervell Court
- **6** Kaldor Court
- **7** Forum Court
- **8** Consul Court
- **9** Ennisdale Close
- A2 **1** Lauriston Place
- **2** Sandwick Close
- **3** Caledon Way
- **4** Augustus Close
- **5** Hercules Close
- **6** Abercorn Place
- **7** Pavilion Court
- **8** Emperor Court
- B2 **1** Bayford Place
- **2** Caravere Close
- **3** Basset Close
- **4** Cobholm Place
- **5** Bagot Place

17
- B1 **1** Lady Margaret Road
- **2** Mount Pleasant Walk
- **3** Mount Pleasant
- **4** Shelly Row
- **5** Albion Yard
- **6** Albion Row
- **7** Haymarket Road
- **8** Castle Row
- **9** Honey Hill
- B2 **1** St Stephen's Place
- **2** St Christophers Avenue
- **3** Priory Street
- **4** Benson Street
- **5** Benson Place
- **6** Prince William Court
- B3 **1** Belmore Close
- **2** Lingholme Close
- **3** Lexington Close
- B4 **1** Blandford Walk
- **2** Chancellors Walk
- **3** Martingale Close
- **4** Farringford Close
- C3 **1** Dalton Road
- **2** Hall Farm Road
- C4 **1** Fordwich Close
- **2** Northumberland Close
- **3** Brackley Close

18
- A2 **1** Springfield Terrace

20
- **1** Rachel Close
- **2** Leonard Close
- **3** Helen Close
- **4** Bergholt Close
- **5** Coggeshall Close
- **6** Brentwood Close
- **7** Chigwell Court

25
- B1 **1** Cenacle The
- **2** Newnham Croft Street
- **3** Grantchester Street
- **4** Lammas Field

26
- A1 **1** Brookside Lane
- **2** Coronation Mews
- **3** Francis Passage
- B1 **1** Claremont
- **2** George Pateman Court
- C2 **1** Wilkin Street
- **2** Angus Close
- **3** Fletcher's Terrace
- **4** Swann's Terrace
- **5** David Street
- C3 **1** Upper Gwydir Street
- **2** Flower Street
- **3** Blossom Street
- **4** Ainsworth Court
- **5** Mackenzie Road
- **6** Bray
- **7** Athlone
- **8** Staffordshire Gardens
- **9** Ashley Court
- C4 **1** Sun Street
- **2** Parker's Terrace
- **3** Wellington Court
- **4** Wellington Street
- **5** St Matthew's Court
- **6** Hollymount
- **7** Donegal
- **8** Enfield
- **9** Carlow

27
- A2 **1** Campbell Street

32
- C1 **1** Lambourn Close
- **2** Southbrooke Close
- **3** Gayton Close
- **4** Beverley Way

34
- C3 **1** Baycliffe Close
- **2** Rothleigh Road
- **3** Limetree Close
- **4** Sycamore Close

35
- A3 **1** Greystoke Court
- **2** Blenheim Close
- **3** Glenacre Close
- B4 **1** Pamplin Court
- **2** Chalfont Close
- **3** Conway Close
- **4** Augers Road
- **5** Daws Close

45
- A2 **1** St Mary's Street
- **2** St Mary's Passage
- **3** Guildhall Street
- **4** St Edwards Passage
- **5** Guildhall Place
- C2 **1** Adam and Eve Street
- **2** Dover Street
- **3** Petersfield

PHILIP'S MAPS
the Gold Standard for serious driving

◆ Philip's street atlases cover every county in England and Wales, plus much of Scotland.

◆ All our atlases use the same style of mapping, with the same colours and symbols, so you can move with confidence from one atlas to the next

◆ Widely used by the emergency services, transport companies and local authorities.

◆ Created from the most up-to-date and detailed information available from Ordnance Survey

◆ Based on the National Grid

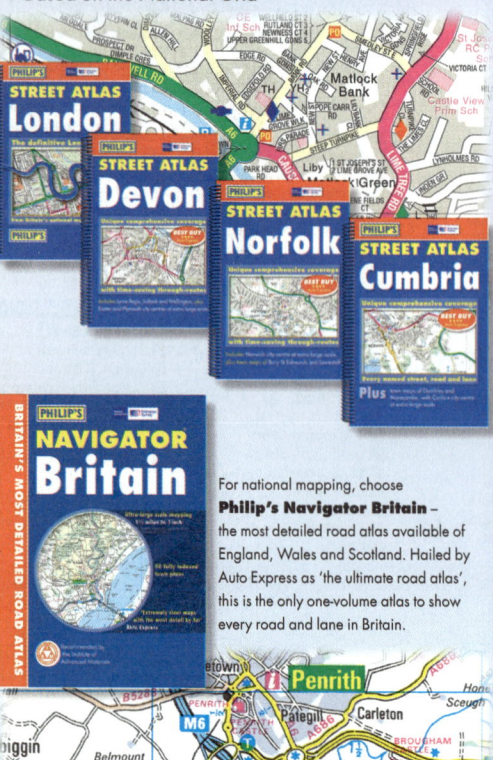

All England and Wales coverage

Street atlases currently available

England
- Bedfordshire
- Berkshire
- Birmingham and West Midlands
- Bristol and Bath
- Buckinghamshire
- Cambridgeshire
- Cheshire
- Cornwall
- Cumbria
- Derbyshire
- Devon
- Dorset
- County Durham and Teesside
- Essex
- North Essex
- South Essex
- Gloucestershire
- North Hampshire
- South Hampshire
- Herefordshire Monmouthshire
- Hertfordshire
- Isle of Wight
- Kent
- East Kent
- West Kent
- Lancashire
- Leicestershire and Rutland
- Lincolnshire
- London
- Greater Manchester
- Merseyside
- Norfolk
- Northamptonshire
- Northumberland
- Nottinghamshire
- Oxfordshire
- Shropshire
- Somerset
- Staffordshire
- Suffolk
- Surrey
- East Sussex
- West Sussex
- Tyne and Wear
- Warwickshire
- Birmingham and West Midlands
- Wiltshire and Swindon
- Worcestershire
- East Yorkshire Northern Lincolnshire
- North Yorkshire
- South Yorkshire
- West Yorkshire

Wales
- Anglesey, Conwy and Gwynedd
- Cardiff, Swansea and The Valleys
- Carmarthenshire, Pembrokeshire and Swansea
- Ceredigion and South Gwynedd
- Denbighshire, Flintshire, Wrexham
- Herefordshire Monmouthshire
- Powys

Scotland
- Aberdeenshire
- Ayrshire
- Edinburgh and East Central Scotland
- Fife and Tayside
- Glasgow and West Central Scotland
- Inverness and Moray
- Lanarkshire

For national mapping, choose **Philip's Navigator Britain** – the most detailed road atlas available of England, Wales and Scotland. Hailed by Auto Express as 'the ultimate road atlas', this is the only one-volume atlas to show every road and lane in Britain.

How to order
Philip's maps and atlases are available from bookshops, motorway services and petrol stations. You can order direct from the publisher by phoning **01903 828503**
or online at **www.philips-maps.co.uk**
For bulk orders only, phone 020 7644 6940